The Joy Thieves

Jennifer Elizabeth Barchi

David Russell Tullock

Parson's Porch BookPublishing & Company

Turning words into books & Turning books into bread

The Joy Thieves
ISBN: Softcover 978-1-946478-17-7
Copyright © 2017 by Jennifer Elizabeth Barchi

All rights reserved. No part of this book may be reproduced or transmitted in any form or by any means, electronic or mechanical, including photocopying, recording, or by any information storage and retrieval system, without permission in writing from the publisher.

All of the Biblical quotations are either from the NRSV or the Good News Bible (only sermons from 2010-2011).

To order additional copies of this book, contact:

Parson's Porch Books
1-423-475-7308
www.parsonsporch.com

Parson's Porch Books is an imprint of **Parson's Porch & Book Publishers** in Cleveland, Tennessee, which has double focus. We focus on the needs of creative writers who need a professional publisher to get their work to market, & we also focus on the needs of others by sharing our profits with those who struggle in poverty to meet their basic needs of food, clothing, shelter and safety.

The Joy Thieves

Contents

Introduction 7
The Muskrat Coat 9
   Deuteronomy 26:1-11; Luke 4:1-13
Repairers of the Breach 14
   Isaiah 58:1-12; Matthew 5:13-20
Get Out of My Boat! 18
   Isaiah 43:1-7; Luke 3:15-17, 21-22
The Things We Carry 23
   Galatians 6:1-10; Matthew 11:16-19, 25-30
Four Tables 29
   Colossians 1:11-20; Luke 1:68-79
How To Build A Fire At High Altitude 34
   Ephesians 4:1-16: Luke 9:28-36
The Love of God Made Flesh 39
   Ephesians 3:1-12; Matthew 2:1-12
Becoming a Pentecostal Church 44
   Ezekiel 37:1-14; Acts 2:1-21
Good Sheep 48
Just before the Baltimore uprising 48
   Psalm 23; John 10:11-18
Lydia 53
   Acts 16:9-21; Revelation 21:10, 21:22-22:5
Life is a Highway 58
   Isaiah 35:1-10
So Stay Here Until… 64
   Luke 24:36b-48 (and 49)
Grave Patience 68
   John 11:17-44; Psalm 30

Stormy with a Chance of Drowning 74
   Matthew 14:22-33
The 'E' Word 79
   Mark 4:1-9; Romans 12:9-21
Mourning Stars 84
   Philippians 2:12-18
Love Is Born at Christmas 90
   Luke 1:26-38; Luke 2:1-20
A Deep and Terrifying Darkness 94
   Genesis 15:1-12, 17-18; Luke 13:31-35
No Lamb Cakes Here 100
   John 20:1-18
The Mustard Seed People 105
   1 Samuel 15:34-16:13; Mark 4:26-34
The Furby in the Pot 111
   1 Samuel 17:1-49
YOLO 116
   Mark 8:27-38
Joy Thieves 121
   Nehemiah 8:1-10; Luke 4:14-21

Introduction

"We don't want a storyteller." The search committee told me this in one of my final interviews, after I asked what they were looking for in a preacher. Their response triggered a sinking feeling in my gut because that's exactly what I am: a storyteller. For a brief moment I thought of writing a completely new sermon to give them as a sample of my style, but common sense won. So it was with great reluctance that I sent them the documents that I'd already prepared. Certainly my homiletic style would take me out of the running for this position that I was so excited about and felt so called to.

Much to my surprise it did not.

Not long after I started serving as the pastor of Dickey Memorial Presbyterian Church, one of the members of that search committee took me aside and said, "You know, when we said we didn't want a storyteller, we weren't talking about *your* kind of stories. We just wanted someone who would challenge and teach us, not just give us fluff."

I understood what she meant. For many adults in America, the word storytelling evokes images of childhood - brightly colored artwork illustrating the fast-paced narratives of picture books or the family Thanksgiving table where Grandma and Grandpa tell the hilarious stories of mom or dad as a kid. Even though we *know* that Jesus' parables were technically stories, we don't always equate modern storytelling with *serious* spiritual growth. Too often we think that *serious* learning should come in an equally serious package.

When I was in seminary, I had the great privilege of taking a class on moral formation through literature. We read and discussed novel after novel discerning how the narrative framework led the reader on a spiritual journey. Our professor, Dr. Osmer, told us that fiction provides a unique opportunity: in fictitious worlds we accompany the characters as they make spiritual, moral, and ethical decisions. Alongside them, *we* get to 'try on' new ways of being, new ways of acting, even new ways of thinking in an environment that is completely safe and non-threatening. It allows us to experiment in ways that we might not otherwise.

For me, this is how the best sermons have operated. The ones that I remember the most clearly from my early days in church are the ones that contained stories in which I could find myself and engage with God. Those sermons are also the ones that have had the most profound impact on my spiritual life as I grew from adolescence into adulthood. And this hasn't changed for me. I still crave homiletic moments where a story draws me into the scripture more deeply or into an encounter with Christ or into an unexpected realization about my spiritual life. And perhaps it is because I crave these so deeply that this is what I tend to write.

What follows is a collection of sermons that are also stories. Most come from the last few years here at Dickey Memorial in Baltimore though a few wormed their way in from a year spent serving a church in Northern Ireland. Some imagine their way into the stories found in scripture, some use stories from my own life or the lives of those I love, and some are fictitious in their entirety. A few are complete narratives; most are only partially so. But they are all, at their core, storytelling sermons.

The Muskrat Coat
Deuteronomy 26:1-11; Luke 4:1-13

Family legend has it that when my uncle Rob was a young man, first dating my aunt Marilyn, he made a particularly striking impression on my grandparents. On the evening in question my grandmother and grandfather were hosting their bridge club – and based on my grandmother's impeccable sense of style, I imagine this to have been a sensible gathering of well-dressed couples with respectable jobs. And I imagine, too, that my grandmother would have been an elegant hostess, warm and jovial but with everything in order and plenty of food to go around.

As the story goes, Rob interrupted this wholesome scene when he knocked on the door to pick up Marilyn for a date. Upon opening the door, my grandmother was surprised to see this young man dressed in a full-length fur coat that looked, shall we say, well-used. It was clear that it wasn't a coat of fine fur – it wasn't beaver or mink or anything classy like that. It was, she thought, muskrat. On top of that my grandmother wasn't entirely sure that it was a *man's* coat. Everyone – including Rob – agrees that he probably looked just a bit ridiculous. But Rob recalls that he was quite proud of that coat. It was a cold winter, and he'd found this warm garment for a very good price at the Goodwill. So he wore it. Now of course, my uncle didn't just wait meekly in the doorway, hiding away the muskrat coat. No, no, he strode into the room where the bridge club was gathered and gave everyone there a huge hug, enveloping them in the well-worn, brown fur.

This is one of my favorite family stories. I love it because it says so much about Rob, whom I adore, but also because it tells me something important about my family. There are plenty of people who, in my grandmother's position, would have shooed Rob out of the house, or at least barred him from the room with all of the bridge players. There are plenty of people who would have been bent out of shape by his appearance. But not my grandparents. My grandparents had a great sense of humor, and they were warm and tolerant people. And that's what I remember when we tell this story as a family. I remember them, and I am reminded that I have the capacity to be like them, because I am their granddaughter, and my identity is bound up in my family's history. After all, that's part of why we tell family stories: to give our children a sense of where they come from – and to give them a sense of who they are. I see this so clearly in my mom. She loves to tell two stories about her parents in particular. First, she recalls her wonder as a small child at her mother's ability to slice a pie into five exactly equal slices – without fail, every time. And second, she tells the story of the time that her dad took her sister to the hardware store to pick up some things for around the house. They had just made it back to the car when her dad realized that the cashier had given him an extra nickel in change. Without pause, my grandfather returned to the store to give the nickel back. My mom will tell you that these stories shaped her sense of fairness, and cultivated her practice of doing the right thing even when no one would notice if you didn't. They became a part of her identity as a member of the Mollman family, and she, in turn, passed them on to my brother and me.

I'm sure that if you took some time to think about it, you would discover family stories – good and bad – that have been passed down from generation to generation to communicate something of your family's values and identity. These narratives shape us, they hold us, and they guide us; they give us insight into who we are, and why we're here. And it strikes me that this has been true for thousands of years.

In our old testament lesson for today, we walk with the Israelites as they approach the altar with their offerings. And we hear that they are commanded to tell *their* family story – the story of their people. "A wandering Aramean was my ancestor; he went down into Egypt and lived there as an alien, few in number, and there he became a great nation, mighty and populous. When the Egyptians treated us harshly and afflicted us, by imposing hard labor on us, we cried to the LORD, the God of our ancestors; the LORD heard our voice and saw our affliction, our toil, and our oppression. The LORD brought us out of Egypt with a mighty hand and an outstretched arm, with a terrifying display of power, and with signs and wonders; and he brought us into this place and gave us this land, a land flowing with milk and honey."

It's a story that tells them who they are, not just as a nation, but in relation to God. It's a story that they will tell over and over so that each generation will have a sense of their corporate identity. They are a people who have seen hardship and lived through it. They are a people whom God has protected and cared for. They have the capacity to flourish, and they come from an Aramean who was incredibly courageous. It also reminds them again and again that God will hear them when they call, and that even when things seem bleak, God will provide. It is perhaps no wonder, then, that many of the Hebrew Scriptures were actually written down during the Babylonian exile. It was during this time of national crisis that the people needed to remember who they were and what God had done for them more than ever. It was during this national crisis that they needed to remember their identity as a people, and as *God's* people. So they collected the stories, and they wrote those stories down.

It strikes me that this narrative lies just beneath the surface when it comes to our passage from Luke. Jesus has been raised as a good Israelite. He has been raised to go to the temple and to say, "A wandering Aramean was my ancestor…" and he *knows* his scripture. He *knows* the stories of his people and his God. His identity as the Son of God is bound up in these narratives. So it shouldn't surprise us that when the devil says, "If you *are* the Son of God, then command this stone to become a loaf of bread," or "If you *are* the son of God, then throw yourself down from here," Jesus responds by quoting scripture. See the devil is challenging his identity. The devil is trying to shake his sense of security about who he is and what he's called to do. But Jesus knows his family stories too well for that. When the devil tempts him to turn a stone to bread to *prove* that he's the Son of God, Jesus can say, "I *am* the Son of God, and I know that humanity doesn't live on bread alone. And I know too that God has always provided for my people. I am secure in the knowledge that God will provide for me." When the devil says, "I'll give you all the kingdoms of the world if you worship me," Jesus can say, "I remember how God gave Moses authority. I remember how God gave the judges and the prophets the power that they needed to live into their call. I don't need to have authority over all the kingdoms of the earth, I just need to worship my God." And when the devil says, "If you are the Son of God, then prove it by throwing yourself off of this tower," Jesus can say, "I *am* the Son of God. I don't need to prove it. And I *know* how God has saved my people in the past – I don't need *God* to prove it to me. Because I *know* the story, and because I *know* where I fit into it, you can't shake my confidence in who I am. You can't tempt me to second guess myself."

Jesus' confidence in this biblical scene always astounds me. It always makes me wish that I were that sure of myself. When I was growing up, and perhaps when you were growing up too, the questions of "Who am I?" and "What am I here for?" bubbled beneath the surface of my life and the lives of my friends. They were huge questions for us – questions that loomed large in our adolescences as we searched for ourselves. And I never felt like I *had* that narrative to help me figure out my identity or my purpose in the world. I never felt like I *had* that confidence that Jesus does.

At least not until I met Pastor Todd. Todd became the pastor at Gladwyne Presbyterian Church a couple of years before I went to seminary. It was him that I met with when my dad first suggested I think about ministry. When I told him that I was skeptical about this whole call thing, he told me to read the book of Jonah. So I did – I read about the reluctant prophet who tried to do the whole running-away-thing. He was moody, depressed, angry. A lot like the young-twenty-something me. I found myself in his story, and it made holy my own struggle with this call that I was hearing.

Up until then, I hadn't spent much time reading the Bible, and I would have said that I didn't think it was that important. But as I made my way through seminary, and as I learned more and more of the narrative of our family of faith, I discovered that there were stories in there that resonated with all of my modern experiences. And those stories reminded me of God's faithfulness, and Christ's promises, and the Spirit's actions. And they did something else, too – they gave me a sense of purpose. God is at work transforming the world into the Kingdom of God. So no matter what my career, my purpose is to contribute to that kingdom-building work in my own way.

I recently asked Lauren what Bible story she remembers resonating with her first. And she said, "The story of Noah and the Ark. Because…animals!" Most of you know that she's an environmental scientist – saving nature is her thing. The story of Noah gave her confidence that that work was holy work. It helped her understand her own calling in the context of what God is doing in the world. Like Noah, she's working to save God's creation from disaster.

The truth is, the scriptures *are* our family history – they *are* the stories of our family of faith. And just like the stories about my uncle or my grandparents help me to understand who I am as part of the Mollman tribe, so does the Bible help us to understand who *we* are as part of God's people and what our purpose is. The better we know these stories, the more secure we feel in our identities as God's children. The better we know these stories, the less we feel we need to prove ourselves when temptation comes knocking. This lent we'll be talking about our personal stories and how they intersect with the biblical stories. So I invite you, in this season, to read – to read the stories of your ancestors in the faith; to read the stories of this family of which you are a part; to learn them as you have learned your own family's stories. I invite you to find yourself in the Bible – to find that you are a father Abraham, called by God to strike out into the unknown, or to find that you are a mother Sarah, laughing at an incredible promise that God has made to you. I invite you to find that you are a leader like Moses, struggling to bring your followers through a very rough time, or to find that you are a Queen Esther, given privilege for the purpose of helping others in just such a time as this. I invite you to find that you are a Peter, stepping out on the waves in faith one moment and then sinking in fear the next, or to find that you are a Thomas, wavering between intense courage and doubt. I invite you to learn the stories and to find yourself within them, that you might go through life confident that you are a child of God, that your life *matters*, and that God is even now continuing the biblical drama and working through *you* to transform this world into Christ's loving and peace-filled kingdom.

Repairers of the Breach
Isaiah 58:1-12; Matthew 5:13-20

Back in November, when the weather was just starting to turn colder, Lauren and I headed down to the Eastern Shore to spend a couple of days at my family's cabin. That Saturday was the first time for the season that it was chilly enough to turn on the heat, which we did just before lunch. As the air started to circulate, we attended to a couple of chores outside. By the time we ventured back inside, it was just starting to warm up, so I started walking through the open kitchen/dining/living space towards the bedroom to take off a layer. But as I passed the peninsula that demarcates the kitchen I saw something out of the corner of my eye – something long and black. It was a snake – perhaps three feet in length – certainly not the biggest I've encountered but big enough. He was slithering slowly along the floorboards in such a way that I thought that he had probably just gotten warm enough to wake up. So I called my fiancée, as you do for dealing with unwanted, nonhuman houseguests, and we stared for a second. Big, black – rat snake, we agreed. And that was great because rat snakes are harmless, and they're honestly usually pretty nice. When I was a kid, my brother and I used to hunt for them on rocks and sunny logs in the summer and hang them around our necks like necklaces. So, we figured, escorting this guy outside was no big deal. We had no ill feelings towards him, and he was certainly dealing with any mice that were in the house. Big win there. Ready to pick him up and gently put him on a sunny spot in the driveway, we approached. And then it happened.

Seeing us, the snake – whom we named Billy – raised his head, and he raised his tail, and he shook it just like a rattler. Game changer. Lauren and I jumped back and ran for weapons and a guidebook. Suddenly, we weren't at ease. Suddenly, we didn't want to be nice. Suddenly, we felt threatened and feared for our safety. Even after we checked the guidebook and found out that rat snakes do, in fact, imitate poisonous snakes to ward off enemies, we were still quite wary. Instead of approaching Billy with gentle kindness, we came with a sponge mop and a broom and brusquely, even aggressively, started pushing him like a hockey puck towards the front door.

Joy Thieves

Cornered with Lauren, Billy started to – I kid you not – climb the wood paneled wall, so Lauren whacked him down and shoved again to get him over the threshold. Then she unceremoniously dumped him off of the deck and into the leaves below. Forget sunny spots. Forget warmth for a cold-blooded creature. Billy scared us, so we had to get rid of him.

Looking back on it, I'm amazed by how quickly my attitude towards him changed when he rattled that tail of his. Looking back on it, I'm amazed by how quickly I went from compassion to anger.

But perhaps I shouldn't be amazed – after all, that's not the first time that's happened to me, and it's not confined to my response to animals.

Shortly after Lauren and I were engaged last year, I reached out to a family that is very dear to me in Northern Ireland. I asked their advice on whether and what I should say to the congregation that I had served there about our engagement. After some time, this family – whom I have loved as my own family – wrote back. They said that, while they were absolutely thrilled for me, they advised against my sharing this piece of news with the church at that time. They cautioned that some people would be hurt; they'd have questions; some might even question my ordination and my call as a minister. Besides, they were in the process of searching for a new pastor themselves, so now was not a good time to break news that would be considered so shocking in their context. It hurt, and it made me feel vulnerable, even like my character was under attack. My immediate reaction was, "Well then I'm not inviting any of them to the wedding, then." See what I did there? Just like with Billy, I went from loving compassion to angry retribution in two seconds flat. Just like with Billy, as soon as I felt threatened, as soon as I was afraid, I lashed out. Maybe you've been there. Maybe you've experienced a situation like that too. I think it's human nature. I think it's hardwired into our brains from the cave-man days when life or death was a daily struggle.

So why bring it up this morning? Well, because we have two scriptures that ask us to think hard about what it means to be a light to the world. We have two scriptures that call us to put our faith into action, to loose the bonds of injustice, to undo the thongs of the yoke, to let the oppressed go free, and to break every yoke. We have two scriptures that affirm the work that we are doing as a congregation and as individuals to work for justice within our own families, our own communities, our cities and our country. We have two scriptures that make it very clear that God calls us to share our bread with the hungry and to bring the homeless poor into our own houses and to cover the naked. We have two scriptures that pull no punches when it comes to what God requires of us – to treat the least among us in this world as if they were Christ himself.

But there is something else that these two scriptures make very clear – in our work for justice we must not give into the temptation to demonize those whom we view as the oppressor. Isaiah says, "Do not hide yourself from your own kin," and then later, "If you remove the yoke from among you, the pointing of the finger, the speaking of evil…then your light shall rise in the darkness." Isaiah, all the while provoking the people to tear down the oppression in their midst, prevents them from pointing fingers or speaking evil or (as I interpret the line about hiding yourself from you own kin) cutting themselves off from those with whom they disagree. Jesus doesn't say, "you need to forget all about the Pharisees;" he says, "you need to *exceed* the Pharisees." He doesn't demonize them, but he urges his disciples to be like them and then outpace them in faith. Isaiah and Jesus call us to be a light in times of darkness; they call us to work for justice, for the fair treatment of all; but they also demand that we do so constructively, without insult, without lashing out at those who are the oppressors, without allowing our own fear to move us to our own acts of injustice. Indeed they urge us to be the ones who will be called the repairers of the breach – they urge us to love even those whom we consider our enemies, that through us the Holy Spirit might bring healing to the nation.

No doubt you will come back and say to me, "But even Jesus called the Pharisees a brood of vipers." And you're right, he did. But he also had a relationship with them. He ate with them. He worshipped in their synagogues. He met with them in the middle of the night to talk theology. Jesus *knew* them. And Jesus *loved* them. Even when they threatened him, Jesus did not back down from his work but he also did not put *them* down.

It seems to me that now, more than ever, the Church has a calling to be the light of the world – and *this* church has a calling to host God's table of reconciliation, to be the repairers of the breach. After all, we are a congregation of democrats and republicans (and independents and libertarians and everything in between). We are a congregation of citizens and immigrants. We are a congregation of whites and blacks. We are a congregation of wealthy and poor. We are a congregation of straight and gay. We are a congregation of old and young. We are a congregation of women and men. We are a congregation that does not always agree. But we are still in relationship with one another. And *that* is what we need to take into the world beyond these walls. It only takes five seconds on Facebook or YouTube to see people tearing each other apart – in the name of justice. We are called to something different. We are called to do justice *while* loving kindness. We are called to seek out relationships with those with whom we disagree so that when they rattle their tails like a poisonous snake, we don't grab for the nearest weapon to beat them into submission. We are called not to cut ourselves off from our kin but to be the repairers of the breach. I know that you all will go out this week and follow Isaiah's command to loose the bonds of oppression and break the yoke of injustice, each in your own way, around the issues that matter to you; I urge you, this week, to also follow our scriptures' command to be a light in the darkness and the light of the world – do not point the finger, and do not speak evil. Love those who inspire anger within you, and pray for those who make you afraid. Do not give in to injustice, but in standing up to injustice do not become the oppressor yourself. Do justice while loving kindness that we might truly be the repairers of the breach and the restorers of streets to live in for *all* of God's children.

Get Out of My Boat!
Isaiah 43:1-7; Luke 3:15-17, 21-22

John answered all of them by saying, "I baptize you with water; but one who is more powerful than I is coming; I am not worthy to untie the thong of his sandals. He will baptize you with the Holy Spirit and fire. His winnowing fork is in his hand, to clear his threshing floor and to gather the wheat into his granary; but the chaff he will burn with unquenchable fire."

I remember hearing this passage when I was in high school, sitting in the small, bright sanctuary of the church right down the street from me. Pastor Helen read the verse, and my mind got stuck on the last little bit: but the chaff he will burn with unquenchable fire. My teenage brain started imagining the winnowing, coming up with a fantastic scene: a whole host of people standing before an enormous Jesus who had fiery eyes and a huge, pointy pitchfork – not unlike the caricatures of the devil that populate cartoons. Some of those in the crowd were drawn close in a big hug, as Christ murmured, "You are my children, my beloved. In you I am so pleased." Others were pushed into a giant furnace by the hands of an angry God. It was a terrifying daydream, in part because the idea of such a messiah – of a messiah who welcomes some and destroys others – was utterly frightening; and in part because, as a teenager, I was pretty certain that I didn't belong in the "wheat" group of people; I was pretty sure I would be considered "chaff." And I had heard enough televangelists and street-corner-preachers in my life explaining that this verse meant that the Lord would separate the good people from the bad that I was pretty certain that I was doomed to an eternity of fire in hell. It so scared me that I didn't even hear what Pastor Helen had to say about it in her sermon. She had read the condemnatory verse; I didn't want to hear anything more that might hurt me, and so I tuned her out. It didn't sound much like 'good news' to me. And so for years, I did my best to ignore this little line from the Bible.

The truth is I didn't have to think much about it again until I got to seminary, which suited me just fine. But we weren't very many weeks into the first semester of our first year when it reared its terrifying, ugly head once more. A small group of us gathered early each morning to do a lectio divina – a meditative reading of the lectionary text. Together we would read the passage three times, listening and reflecting on a word or a phrase that stuck out to us, the emotion that the text evoked, and how God might be calling us through those words that day. On the morning when this gospel text from Luke came up, it just so happened that Adam was with us. Adam was a second-career student. He was in his thirties and had spent the better part of the last decade working on Wall Street. He had quit his job to go to seminary just before the recession hit, a coincidence that he thanked God for on a regular basis as his former coworkers found themselves without work.

On this particular morning, when we got to the second time reading through the passage – the reading for emotion – Adam said, "You know, this text makes me feel really grateful. I am really grateful that Christ is so patient with us as he throws the chaff into the unquenchable fire." And I must have been giving him a really incredulous look because he very quickly continued. "I first felt the call to go to seminary right after I graduated from college. But I had been offered a job in New York making a salary that I wouldn't have thought possible right out of school. My friends were in the city, and I could live the way that I had always thought I wanted to – I could keep living like I was in college, only with money. There was no way I was giving that up to become a pastor," he said. And then he went on to describe that moment when he made the decision to say no to God's call.

The pastor of his church agreed to meet with him, and Adam laid out the situation. He confessed that he felt the call and that members of the congregation seemed to sense it too – they kept encouraging him to take that leap of faith. One member had even said to him, "It's like Jesus has found you out in your boat on the ocean. And he's gotten into your boat with you, and he's telling you that over that horizon is a land you're really gonna love; you just need to follow the course that he plots for you." Adam admitted to his pastor that all he wanted to do was to say to Jesus, "Get out of my boat!" Because here was the truth: going to seminary would mean giving up a lot. It wasn't so much about the money, though as a young-20-something with college debt, the money mattered. But it was also giving up his friends, leaving the people that he'd grown to love and the social gatherings that made him so happy. He didn't want to do it. He didn't want to give up so much.

And his pastor said to him, "Then tell Jesus to get out of your boat. It's not like Christ is going to abandon you if you don't go to seminary. It's like God said to the people of Israel, 'I will be with you when you pass through the waters, and I will protect you when you walk through fire because I love you, and you are mine.' God will be with you and will bless you either way, because you are God's, and God loves you."

So Adam told Jesus to get out of his boat, and he stayed on Wall Street for more than a decade. The call didn't go away, though, and each year the work that he was doing grew more and more unfulfilling, and each year he grew more and more uncomfortable with the corporate culture in which he was immersed, and each year he felt a little bit more ready to move away from a social circle that still operated like it had on his college campus, until finally he was ready to say yes.

Which brought him to that morning with us. And he said, "It took that Holy Spirit and fire that Jesus gave me at my baptism ten years to burn away the chaff in me that kept me from taking this step. But God was patient, and God didn't leave me, and God just kept working on me. And I am really grateful for that."

I had never considered the possibility that John meant that both the wheat and the chaff were in *us* – I'd always thought that John was saying that people are either wheat *or* chaff, either bad or good. I had never considered the possibility that John might be talking about the promise made to us in our baptism – that God gives us the Holy Spirit and throughout our lives that Spirit is at work in us to grant us ever deeper joy and to make us ever more Christ-like. I had never considered the possibility that this text from Luke might not have been intended as a weapon to threaten people with hell, but might instead have truly been intended as the good news that Christ will help us grow into our best selves – our most 'wheat-y' selves – no matter how many times we dig in our heels, no matter how many times we turn away, no matter how many times we tell Jesus to get out of our boats.

All of this popped to the fore of my mind last Sunday evening. Lauren and I had decided to tackle the project of organizing the third floor in the manse. In all honesty, before then it looked sort of like a paper mill had exploded, and my policy was pretty much to avoid it at all costs. But it's a new year, so we took it on, and in the process of sorting papers we came across a note that one of my high school students had written to me the year that I did youth ministry before seminary. I had asked her to pay attention to the negative things that she told herself, and she'd created a list. It included things like, 'I'm unforgiveable,' 'God can't possibly love me – I'm too bad a person,' and 'I'm going to hell.' I wish I could say that I hardly ever heard people say these things about themselves. But the truth is, that youth was more the rule than the exception. As I was reading this piece of paper, we heard our old dog Cyrus start to bark his very annoyed bark downstairs. So we rushed down to find our new dog, Cinnamon, trying to play with him. Now Cinnamon is about a year old - still a puppy really. Someone before us adopted her when she was 10 weeks, but after several months they returned her to the shelter because they couldn't deal with some of her behavior. And she cowers when you get upset with her. She was already cowering when we came downstairs because in the process of trying to play she had flattened Cyrus. And because I'm protective of him I rushed over and said to her, "No! Bad dog!" That's it, just words, but she seemed terrified. I admit that I said it without thinking much of it – good dog, bad dog, is how we trained the first puppy I ever had in my life. But having read this letter from my student and seeing her behavior I paused, and I thought to myself 'but she's not a bad dog – she just doesn't understand, yet, that Cyrus can't play.' And then I thought, she's probably scared that *we're* going to take her back to the shelter too.

I've been thinking about this all week – turning over Adam and that letter and Cinnamon and this text, and you know…I think that we have a good dog/bad dog problem. Somehow in our society we've developed a theology that says that we're either good people or we're bad people, and that God is either with us or God is ready to take us back to the pound, to throw us into the unquenchable fire. We're either ready to follow God *right now* and we're righteous, or we tell God to get out of our boats and we're unrighteous. But the truth of our texts this morning is something very different – the truth of our texts this morning is the truth that Adam shared with us in seminary. The truth is that we're people created in God's good image who sometimes make poor decisions or who sometimes need time to make the healthy decision. We are good wheat, but there's chaff hanging on, and sometimes that chaff obscures the image of Christ within us. But God's promise is this: that no matter what, God loves us. No matter what, God stays with us to burn the chaff away. No matter what, God claims us as God's own, and God will never abandon us, God will never take us back to the pound, God will never cast us into the unquenchable fire for all of eternity. God in Christ points us back to the waters of baptism and says, "When you pass through the waters I am with you; when you walk through the fires you shall not be burned. I give you my Spirit to burn through your chaff that you might follow me and have abundant joy. And no matter how many times you tell me to get out of your boat, I will abide with you until you can hear me saying, 'you are my beloved child, and I am so pleased with you.'"

The Things We Carry
Galatians 6:1-10; Matthew 11:16-19, 25-30

"Come to me all you that are weary and are carrying heavy burdens, and I will give you rest." To my mind as a teenager, this could have been the advertising slogan to sell Christianity to the masses. "Come to me all you weary people, and I will give you rest!" It sounded like the miracle drug—come to Christ and *bam*, the weariness was gone and rest was guaranteed! I could see the advertisement in my head: the perfect warm, sunny day with just a gentle breeze and a hammock stretched between two trees. And in the midst of the drama and trauma of a new school and a tense family and fickle friends that kind of rest was *exactly* what I was looking for. So I started going to church and quickly found out what all of you probably know quite well—it wasn't an overnight quick fix that took all of my burdens away. Was this false advertising? Or was Jesus talking about a different kind of rest altogether—something much deeper than a lazy sort of life without any cares or troubles—the kind of rest that restores your soul even in the midst of life's trials and tribulations?

We can probably all agree upon the latter—that the rest that Jesus promised was something more life-giving than a doze in a hammock. But before we can delve into the question of what such rest in Christ looks like, I think we first need to explore what it means to be weary and carrying heavy burdens.

When I hear the word 'weary,' I can't help but think of the time we took a group of youth canoeing in the Boundary Waters that separate the US from Canada. It was an amazing trip, don't get me wrong, but it gave me a new understanding of the concept of exhaustion. One day in particular, we *had* to get to a campsite on the other side of a large lake. The weather was miserable, on the colder side with rain driven by strong winds over the expanse of the water. The other adult in our group, who had more canoeing experience than I did, told us to stay close to the shore line, but we were finding it difficult. The wind would grab our boats and try to pull us off course. If we didn't paddle continuously, we were sure to drift into the middle of the lake, dauntingly far from where we needed to go. After more than an hour of this slow going, with the wind and the rain chilling us to the bone, our shoulders sore and our arms numb, my canoe-mate and I found ourselves stuck, caught on a log that had been lurking just under the surface. We were getting pulled out to the center of the lake, no matter how furiously we paddled, and I could feel my exhaustion rising to the point of frustrated tears. I knew that we couldn't stop without getting separated from our group, but I didn't feel like we could go on. With the strong wind and our aching arms it just seemed so hopeless.

The thing is, I've felt that hopeless, frustrated, on the verge of giving up or giving in feeling before at times that have had nothing to do with physical exhaustion, and I imagine most of you have as well. They're those times in life when you're working *so hard* to build something good in this world, but every time you make progress forward there's some new obstacle in your way and all that you've accomplished gets toppled—the currents of life pull you backwards. It's like when you put all of your energy into rebuilding a relationship with an estranged loved one and you do everything right—apologizing for the ways in which you've hurt them, extending grace for the ways in which they've wronged you, being willing to listen, to help, to be patient—and at every turn they reject your best efforts, throwing your kindness back in your face. Or it's like when you strive in everything you do to maintain your integrity, to be honest and work to make the world into a better place, but you never seem to get ahead, your plans never seem to work out, while the people who you know cut corners and look out only for their own best interest are living the high life, their dreams turned into reality. Eventually, the work of it all drains you practically dry; you don't want to give up but you can't possibly see a way forward. It's like you're trying to move in one direction but everything in the world is working against you and you feel weary to the bone. When it comes to Jesus' promise of rest, this is the first kind of weariness that we experience, the weariness that comes from fighting against the tides of life.

But that day of hard paddling wasn't the only exhausting part of our trip to the Boundary Waters. See, not all of the lakes were connected to one another; sometimes you had to cross a bit of land to get to the next waterway. I dreaded the days that we came to these. When we arrived, we'd pull the canoes up on shore, empty all of the gear out of them, then hoist the canoes onto our shoulders and begin trekking to the other side of the terrain. These treks took us up steep hills, through patches of marsh where we found ourselves attacked by leeches, and once along a treacherous bit of rocky ups and downs that had most of my youth sitting on boulders beside the trail for a rest long before they finished the journey. The boats were heavy, weighing us down and even when we made it to the other side, we knew that we'd have to go back and get the rest of the gear. By the time we were finished moving from one shore to the next, the weight of the things we carried had taken its toll, and we barely had the energy to keep paddling onward.

In life, too, I believe that it is the things that we carry that are the second cause of our weariness. I never thought that I'd bring up Greek mythology in a sermon, but I have to admit that it sometimes does a brilliant job of capturing human nature. You may perhaps be familiar with the story of Atlas—he was the one who was forced to hold the globe of the heavens on his shoulders. But there was one little trick to this punishment—if someone offered to take the globe from him, he could give up his burden. Now we all might think, who would be stupid enough to do something like that? The thing is most of us do it on a day to day basis; we willingly walk up to the proverbial Atlas and take the weight of the heavens on our shoulders. We often experience it as anger or guilt or stress, but if we look just a little bit below the surface we find that there is the underlying expectation that it all depends on us to be perfect, to be righteous, to keep the world in motion. For me, it is not uncommon for anger at another person to be the particular weight I'm carrying; and sometimes I feel as though it's holding me captive. I wonder why I can't just forgive the person who wronged me and move on. But when I really dig into the whole mess of my rage, I find that there's a little voice in my head that says "anger is not the way a Christian should feel." And so I bottle up all those emotions and never let them see the light of day; I try not to admit that I get angry at all. So it's not just the weight of anger that I'm carrying, but also the weight of trying to be the perfect Christian. And the same is true of guilt and stress. We don't just bear the weight of shame, but also the weight of trying to make ourselves righteous again. We don't just bear the weight of too many responsibilities, but also the weight of holding our families together or keeping our workplaces running smoothly. We may not say it, but somewhere deep down there is the fear that if we were to drop our burden, the world might fall apart just a little. And so we allow the things that we carry to weigh us down, to drain us of energy as we move through our lives.

And Jesus looks at all of us with the things that we carry fighting the tides of life and says, "come to me all you who are weary and heavy burdened and I will give you rest." And it's what we so long for; it's part of the reason we gather here each Sunday. But we also know it's not simple and so we wonder, "what does rest in Christ really look like?"

The rest that Christ offers us is a rich and multi-faceted gift, one that I wouldn't pretend to be able to capture in a single sermon. But there are two aspects of it that I particularly want to highlight. When we were in that canoe, trying to fight our way back to the shoreline, I kept going because I *knew* that as hard as it was we were making progress—we would eventually make it. In life, there are no such guarantees. We do our part to make the world a better place, and most of the time it doesn't seem to make even a dent. We wonder if our best efforts are even worth it. Does it matter if we try to mend that broken relationship? Does it matter if we try to act with integrity? If the answer is no, then it is only natural that we should give in to our weariness. But if the answer is yes, if those efforts of ours *do* matter, if we could be sure that we were making progress even if we couldn't see it, that knowledge itself would give us the energy to keep moving forward. And that knowledge is exactly the kind of rest that Christ offers us. Part of the promise of the resurrection is that the Kingdom of God has been assured, that the Spirit is working *in this world* to bring about that glorious day when there will no longer be crying or pain or suffering, when our broken relationships will be mended, when we will love each other as brothers and sisters. Our efforts here and now, striving against the tides of greed and injustice, brokenness and hatred, they are all part of the Spirit's work. And though it may at times be difficult—even impossible—to see, we can be assured that our striving is not in vain, that eventually our efforts will transform this world as God has promised. In Galatians, Paul encourages us not to tire of doing good; the rest that Christ offers us, that enables us to go on, is the sure knowledge that the good that we do really *does* matter.

But while such knowledge might revive us in the midst of our fighting against the tides of life, it doesn't do much to lighten the burden of the things we carry. And when he's talking about rest, Jesus goes on to say, "Take my yoke upon you and learn from me." Now I don't know about you, but with all that I'm carrying already, the *last* thing that I want is a yoke around my neck—that just sounds like another burden! What on earth is Jesus talking about here? The thing of it is, this might be the most vital lesson that we have to learn; for those of us who willingly take the weight of the world on our shoulders, this might just give us the perspective we need to truly find rest. If we imagine a farmer yoking his oxen to a plow, we think of those oxen as joining in the farmer's work, playing their part in making that man's fields grow. I don't think any of us would think of it the other way around, as the farmer joining in the work of the oxen. Yet, when it comes to Christ that's often exactly the way that we see it; our attitude is one of inviting Christ into *our* tasks and activities, instead of properly seeing all that we do as an extension of the work that Christ is already doing. When Christ invites us to take his yoke upon our shoulders, he is inviting us to join in his work in this world, to join in the building of his Kingdom. The fact of the matter is, it is not Christ who enters into *our* work, but we who enter into *Christ's* work. And if that is the case, then the weight of the world is *never* resting on our shoulders; it rests on the shoulders of God alone. And this is good news of rest indeed, because it means that the responsibility for perfection, for making people righteous, for holding the world together lies with God and God alone. For those of us carrying anger, it allows us to begin giving up the need to be 'perfect' and start expressing how we feel, trusting that God can bring us to a place of forgiveness. For those of us carrying guilt, it allows us to begin letting go of the need to make ourselves righteous, trusting that God is already working in us to bring about that change. And for those of us carrying stress, it allows us to begin letting go of the feeling that everything depends on us, trusting that it really all depends on God. By inviting us to take on his yoke, Christ is offering us the opportunity to set down the things that we carry, to be our imperfect selves and join in his perfect work. And the irony of it is, the more we let go of the burdens that we carry, the longer we are yoked to Christ, realizing that we are joining in *his* fight against the hellish tides of this world, the more we begin to look like the righteous people we were striving to be in the first place. And that is the true rest in Christ indeed.

Four Tables
Colossians 1:11-20; Luke 1:68-79

I bet most of us can remember a time – probably when we were in early elementary school – when our teachers told us the story of that first Thanksgiving in the 1600's. We colored in pictures of that first Thanksgiving table, with pilgrims in tall black hats and black shoes with silver buckles on one side and Native Americans in feathered headdresses and deer skin clothing on the other. There was a turkey on that table and a cornucopia overflowing with fruit and vegetables. It was a hard year, we were told, and the new settlers had trouble finding food in this land that they had taken as their home. They might have starved had it not been for a tribe of Native Americans who helped them to hunt and to grow crops, who showed them how to survive in their new home. So when the fall rolled around and the harvest came, the settlers and the Natives shared in a harvest meal, celebrating together the bounty of the earth.

It's a wonderful story, and it's not without truth. The Wampanoag tribe did teach a group of settlers seeking religious asylum in America how to grow corn and use fish to fertilize their fields. Early in 1621, the Wampanoag and the settlers signed an agreement vowing to protect one another. And in the Autumn, there was a great harvest feast that the Wampanoag and settlers shared together. It spanned over three days, included a great deal of eating, singing, dancing and even the playing of ball-games.

But as beautiful a portrait as this story paints of two different people coming together in peace to share in the blessings of life, we know it's not the end of the story. It wouldn't be too much longer before the European settlers were at odds with the Native Americans. It wouldn't be too much longer before their relationship was marked with bloodshed and deception. It wouldn't be too much longer before the American landscape was shaped by a Trail of Tears.

In many ways, that first table that we drew and colored in grade school was a picture of the promise of what could have been – the way we perhaps wish things *had* been. That first Thanksgiving in 1621 showed that people as different as the Wampanoag and the settlers *could* live and work together in peace, that they could farm the land and raise their children in harmony – side by side, each looking out for the welfare of the other. And I wonder if we don't hold on to that first Thanksgiving table as a sign of hope and longing. That table tells us about who we can be at our best, it tells us about what this nation, this world, even, could be at its best, and so even as we look back on that 1621 meal with nostalgia we also lift it up as the goal towards which we are striving. We long for the community, the mutuality that it represents; we long for the nations, for *our* nation, to be at peace as our ancestors were for those three days of feasting. And yet we know that we aren't there yet. Things have fallen apart since then. And so that first table is colored with promise and pain – the promise of the way things could be and the pain of knowing that our reality is a ways off from that hopeful vision.

In this respect our own Thanksgiving tables are similar to that first table. For ours, too, are tables of hope and longing; they're tables of promise and pain. Whenever Thanksgiving approaches and I begin to think of family gathered around the table, it's Norman Rockwell's iconic painting that flashes into my head. If you're not familiar with it, it's a portrait of multiple generations seated at a long table, the mother just setting down the turkey, the father behind her ready to carve. All the faces that you can see are smiling – and even those that you can't see, you can tell they're smiling too, just from the way the eyebrows are curved or the way the cheeks are pulled upward. The whole scene is perfectly idyllic. It's the entire family together at peace with one another sharing in the bounty of God's creation. It's what we all wish our families would look like as we gather around the Thanksgiving table.

But the truth is, for many of us, reality falls short of what we might wish. For my family, the reality is that we often aren't together when Thanksgiving dinner rolls around. Since my parents' divorce, my brother and I often are with my dad and step mom on this particular holiday, which is wonderful but it means that we miss our mom and her whole side of the family. And she certainly misses us. Now that my brother has moved to California, it's getting harder for him make it to the East Coast for *any* of the holidays, so this year we'll miss him too. Our Thanksgiving table will be beautiful and it will be overflowing and there will be lots of love shared – but it will also be a table of longing. Because it will be a reminder of the distance that separates us; it will be a reminder of relationships that have been broken; it will be a reminder that we are not quite the idyllic portrait that Norman Rockwell depicted. And I wish we were.

Your family's Thanksgiving table likely looks much different than mine, but I imagine that for most of you gathered here today, there's some longing at your table as well. Some families will gather and there will be a chair that stands empty – the seat of someone who has died or fallen ill, the seat of someone who is absent from this year's meal. There's longing as we gaze upon that chair, longing for that person who is no longer with us. Some families will gather and a fight will break out; harsh and hurtful words will be traded between siblings or spouses or parents and children. There's longing as we listen to those tirades, longing for peace and reconciliation between two people that are supposed to love each other. Some families will gather and seated around that table they will look almost exactly like that Norman Rockwell painting – with genuine smiling faces and a table overflowing. But there's longing there too. There's longing because someone present has a dream that's gone unfulfilled. There's longing because someone is growing old and doesn't have the energy that they used to. There's longing because even though everything is joyous within the walls in here, there's a world out there that's in turmoil, and we know we can't escape from its chaos forever.

So our Thanksgiving tables, like that first Thanksgiving table, are tables filled with both hope and longing. There is much hope as we eat together with family and reflect on all of the blessings that we've received – and there is much hope as we hold on to that picture of all the promise that families hold: the promise of love and of relationship; the promise that there are those who know us and accept us just as we are; the promise that there will always be a place that we call home. But there is longing too – because we do not live in a perfect world, and we do not have perfect families. There is longing when we see broken relationships and longing when we are caught in the grip of grief. There is longing when our families don't quite live into the promise that they hold. Yes, our Thanksgiving tables are glorious juxtapositions of hope and longing.

But our Thanksgiving tables are not the only tables that hold together the promise of the universe as it was created to be and the reality of the world as it is. This table that stands in our midst every Sunday, Christ's table, it too is a place where the glorious juxtaposition of hope and longing, of promise and reality, resides. And it too is a table of thanksgiving – that's what the word Eucharist means – thanksgiving. For the meal that we celebrate here each month, it too is a thanksgiving meal, a meal where we give thanks for the gifts that Christ has given us: the bread of life, the cup of salvation. It's a meal where we celebrate and offer our gratitude for the new and abundant life that God gave us by walking in our human shoes, dying and rising once again. Yes, it is a thanksgiving meal and it holds all of the promise of Christ's kingdom. For as we gather around this table, we aren't just looking back at that last meal that Jesus shared with his friends, we're also getting a glimpse of the promised banquet that is to come – the banquet where we'll all sit down together – enemies and friends alike – and share in the richness of God's blessing. Not a mouth will go hungry, no one will thirst, there will be no one who cannot afford bread nor anyone who is not welcome at the table. That's the hope, that's the promise, that we experience and taste at this table. That's the hope, that's the promise, that we glimpse as we gather here.

The thing is, it's just a taste, it's just a glimpse. It's just a moment of getting to see that glorious banquet that is to come. And then we return to this world as it is – where there are still those who hunger, still those who thirst, still those who are enemies, still those who are unwelcome. So this, too, is a table of longing – for just as we long for the healing of our nation, the healing of all of the nations, the healing of our families, so too do we long for the healing of creation. We long for the promise that this table holds. We long for that promised day when what we glimpse here will be made reality.

But friends, this is not just Thanksgiving Sunday, it is also Christ the King Sunday. It's the Sunday when we rejoice that Christ is *our* King. It's the Sunday when we celebrate that Christ's kingdom already *is*. As our Luke passage says, "by the tender mercy of our God, the dawn from on high has broken upon us, to give light to those who sit in darkness and in the shadow of death, to guide our feet into the way of peace." As our passage from Colossians says, "God has rescued us from the power of darkness and transferred us into the kingdom of his beloved Son, in whom we have redemption, the forgiveness of sins."

Now, you might be thinking – didn't you *just* say that that's what we're longing for? That's the promised kingdom that we hope for but that isn't here yet? How can you say that Christ's kingdom already *is*? Well, it's sort of like being a dual citizen. Just because you live in one country, doesn't make the other country any less real. We are dual citizens – citizens of this world and of Christ's kingdom. And just because we live here doesn't make God's kingdom any less *real*. In a sense it is already, but not yet – it's already a reality, but it's not yet fully realized. That banquet table – Christ's banquet table – where we all have a place, where relationships are healed, where not a tear is shed, where no one suffers, where all are fed…that table is already truth. It already exists. And sometimes, sometimes we can see it breaking into this world as it is. We know that we see it here at this Eucharistic table. You could certainly see it at that first Thanksgiving table in 1621. And you can see it this week at your family's Thanksgiving table too. It shines through in the quiet moments when you speak words of gratitude. It shines through in the boisterous moments when everyone doubles over in laughter. It shines through when you tell the stories of those who have died and they are, for a moment, sitting beside you as words bring them to life. It shines through when siblings put aside differences and pass the green beans without bickering. It shines through in a thousand tiny ways.

So gathered around tables with family and friends this week, let us rejoice and give thanks for all of the ways we see Christ's banquet table shining through. And as we gather around this table every month let us rejoice and give thanks that in bread and cup we see Christ's banquet table shining through. And as we gather around every table, this week and every week, whether at work or at home, whether near or far, let us rejoice and give thanks for the ways that we see Christ's banquet table shining through. Yes, let us rejoice and give thanks *always*, for we are citizens already of Christ's kingdom and by the tender mercy of our God, the dawn from on high has broken upon us. Thanks be to God!

How To Build A Fire At High Altitude
Ephesians 4:1-16: Luke 9:28-36

Last Friday, Lauren, Jackson and I got off the trails and headed back to our campsite around five. We were waiting for Nicole to arrive, and we wanted to be there to greet her, especially since we weren't at the campground where we'd planned to camp for the weekend. To pass the time we thought we'd get the fire going and start prepping for dinner. So Jackson and Lauren started to unpack food and cut the watermelon, and I turned my attention to fire-building. Now before I go further, there is something you need to know: the three of us…we're all pretty experienced with building fires. Jackson was a boy scout with plenty of camping experience. Lauren has been building fires since she was a teen, if not before. And I lived in Ireland where the fireplace is a staple method of heating. So we were all pretty confident in our abilities as far as this aspect of camping was concerned.

Round one: my turn. I started with good kindling – lint rolled in newspaper under twigs and sticks that we'd collected earlier. Then I used the teepee method of arranging the logs. We were golden. What could go wrong? So Lauren came over and lit the newspaper, and we all watched as the twigs caught. Perfect! They sizzled and cracked and started to heat up the logs such that they blackened and smoked. It looked like a major success.

It wasn't. About 15 minutes later, we were staring at cold, charred wood, annoyed.

Round two. Lauren's turn. We found more twigs, and we wrapped more newspaper-lint rolls. We started the fire again, but this time Lauren kept adding kindling to keep the temperature up. After all, for a good fire you need heat, oxygen and fuel. It was a bit of a cool evening so maybe we were low on the heat part of the equation. Lauren fed, and she fed, but by the time six o'clock rolled around we were looking once more at a pile of blackened sticks that seemed to have no intention of catching on fire.

Round 3. Jackson's turn. By this point we were theorizing even more about why the fire simply would not start. Perhaps the wood was wet – it certainly seemed to be sizzling a lot. Perhaps we were at a high enough altitude that it needed more oxygen. Perhaps our teepee construction was ill-advised. So I said, "Log Cabin!" and Jackson nodded. That's what he had been thinking too. Very carefully, he rearranged the logs, making out of them a square cabin structure. He put the kindling inside and Lauren lit it. Then he was off to supply a steady stream of twigs. Lauren started blowing on it like a bellows, and when I realized that that seemed to be working, I joined her. The minutes passed by, and still Jackson fed it and Lauren and I puffed. Around seven, Nicole arrived to find us still in those same spots. She played the most vital role of us all – she offered us hungry people sour gummy worms. With the four of us working on it, each with different ideas and different skills, it only took two hours to get the fire going well enough that we could cook dinner. It's a long time, I know, but imagine what would have happened if any one of us had been by ourselves. We'd have starved.

Eventually, once the food made it to my brain, it occurred to me that maybe this was what Paul was talking about when he wrote to the Ephesians and said, "I therefore, the prisoner in the Lord, beg you to lead a life worthy of the calling to which you have been called, with all humility and gentleness, with patience, bearing with one another in love, making every effort to maintain the unity of the Spirit in the bond of peace." Maybe he was telling them to maintain the unity of the body of Christ because, just like the four of us camping, the Ephesians needed each other to live into their calling. Perhaps God calls us to unity in community because we all have different gifts, and we need to use all of those gifts together in order for us to work towards the Kingdom of God. As Paul wrote to the Corinthians in an earlier letter – we are many members of one body, given different gifts for the good of the whole. We cannot say to each other, I have no need of you because without each other, we don't get very far.

Yes, our tale of trying to build a campfire at a (relatively) high altitude did seem to illustrate why Paul called for unity in his letter to the Ephesians. Except…except you've all heard that sermon before. A lot. And for all that it is *true* – we certainly do need to put our gifts together to serve God's kingdom – it somehow falls a bit flat for me, as if it were only *part* of what Paul was getting at in this passage from Ephesians.

If we imagine our way into Paul's shoes, in his time and context, we might discover something deeper. Remember that when he was writing this letter to the Ephesian church, Christianity was still relatively young. Though the number of those who followed Christ was growing, it's not like there was a church on every corner. It's not like you could go church shopping – as many do these days – to find the congregation with exactly your taste in music or your views on politics or your style of worship. Instead, you found yourself part of a community that had individuals very different from you, who might be challenging to get along with, and with whom you might have very little in common. So Paul's call to unity, his call to bear with one another, it's a call to learn how to love and work alongside people whom you may not even like. It's not *just* the feel-good message that we all have gifts, and we can accomplish incredible things in God's service when we use those gifts together; it's also the acknowledgment that living in community is *hard*. It takes work, *real* work. We have to be patient; we have to work through our annoyance, our anger, even our hurt when someone within the community wrongs us. It takes a commitment to *not* walk away when the community as a whole or another member does something that we don't agree with or we don't like, but to instead stay and work for reconciliation, understanding, and mutual growth.

"But here's the promise," says Paul, "The promise is that if we do this hard work of being in community then we will grow *together* into the full stature of Christ." We will become more and more Christ-like ourselves, and as a community we will reflect Christ's love and light with greater and greater intensity. If we *commit* to community, we might just witness a miraculous transformation.

The problem is, we live in a culture that no longer values that commitment.

After my parents got separated, I remember being in Saint Louis with my mom for some family event. She and her sister and I were in my grandparents' kitchen, and mom and Aunt Marilyn were reminiscing about their early years when they shared a bedroom. They would stay up late and pretend that they were saleswomen, selling off their jewelry to one another. After a pause in the conversation my mom said to me, "I wish that I'd raised you and Jon in a smaller house. I think we would have all been closer – none of us could have gone off to our own space and ignored everyone else. We would have had to talk about our problems." At the time, the very idea of living in a smaller house with my big brother made me cringe a little – Jon and I weren't very close – but as I've gotten older, I've come to believe that she was right. I think my family would look much different today if we'd been forced to work through our conflicts and talk instead of running away.

The problem is, we live in a society that encourages us to retreat to our own corners, to our own groups of people who think just like us, instead of working towards unity. Consider congress, for example – instead of working towards compromise, it seems our leaders (and many of us) would rather put all of their energy into ensuring that more people just like them get elected. But wouldn't our country be healthier if we had a diversity of viewpoints in leadership all working together for unity? And consider social media: for all of its benefits (and there are many), it allows us – especially the youngest among us – to surround ourselves with people who think just like we do instead of facing the challenges of real, in person, unpredictable community that we can't just turn off with the flip of a switch. Wouldn't we be healthier if we were consistently confronted by the challenge of working for unity alongside those who do *not* think the way we do? And consider our denominations: when we have major theological disagreements over who should or should not be ordained, or over what we should or should not do or say in regards to issues of justice, or over how we approach worship and the Bible, what do we do? Recently, we've been doing a lot of splitting. We've been doing a lot of what my brother and I did growing up – running to opposite ends of the house and slamming our doors. Wouldn't we be a better Christian witness if we chose to stick together and allow room for the Holy Spirit to move us to reconciliation? And how miraculous, how counter-cultural it would be for us to show the world that God really can work within people to bring them together in spite of deeply held differences in belief. How miraculous it would be to see disciples transform and grow as they doggedly commit to being in community with those who do not think as they do. How miraculous it would be to see so many people becoming more and more Christ-like.

On the second night of our camping trip last weekend – round four with the fire – it was Nicole's turn to give fire-building a go. And wouldn't you know it, the fire was raging in ten minutes, hallelujah, thanks be to God! We ate well, we roasted marshmallows, and then we sat and did our evening devotion. I read the passage from Luke that we read this morning – disciples on a mountaintop witnessing the glory of God. So I asked this: where have you witnessed God's glory on our mountain trip? I expected answers about nature, about endurance. But that's not what I got. Nicole said, "I wasn't sure what to expect on this trip. I was apprehensive about how I would fit in – I don't really know any of you, and I haven't really been to church that much. I kinda thought I'd be the odd one out. But I came anyway, and I see the glory of God in us – in the way that we've so quickly been brought together as a cohesive group." It took me a minute to pick my jaw up off of the floor, but she was absolutely right. Jackson and Lauren echoed that sentiment. We had committed to community that weekend, and the Spirit had done something miraculous among us, knitting us together as one body, growing us in Christ's love and light.

This is the promise to all of us – this miraculous unity, this growing in Christ – so let us commit to one another that we might see God's glory in *our* midst.

The Love of God Made Flesh
Ephesians 3:1-12; Matthew 2:1-12

It started before I even arrived at the airport. At 6:30 on Christmas morning, my phone buzzed – it was a text message from Southwest Airlines informing me that my flight would be 2 hours delayed. Unfortunately, I was carpooling with two other pastors whose flights were still on time, so at 6:45 I was on my way to a long wait at BWI. By the time we made it through security and the other two pastors were safely on board their waiting planes, my estimated time of departure had been pushed back another hour. By the time I was supposed to be landing in Kansas City, we were scheduled to be yet another hour late. Needless to say, by the time I actually arrived, my mom and I only just made it to dinner with my aunt and uncle.

The next day, my mom and I were looking forward to an easy drive to Colorado, followed by a week of fun with my mom's extended family. Yet with our break in Colby, on the western side of the state of Kansas, came the first hint that this trip might not go as smoothly as we'd hoped. When we stopped for gas (at the *one* gas station that we saw), there were long lines for the pumps and a multiplicity of people who felt that they didn't need to wait like nice polite people, but rather had the right to cut in front of everyone else. Once we got to the pump, the squeegee used to wash the windshield was dry as a bone, and there were no others in sight; bad news for a windscreen covered with salt. The hot chocolate machine inside spit out nothing but hot water, and the McDonald's next door was cleaning *their* mocha machine. That's right – there was NO HOT CHOCOLATE in *all* of Colby.

By the time we got back on the road again, it was snowy and the road was icy. As we crossed the Colorado state line, we watched in horror as the two cars in front of us started losing control on black ice that none of us had seen. We could feel our tires lose traction, and we began to careen sideways along I-70. Despite my mom's exceptional driving and our Subaru's exceptional all wheel drive, there was no recovering – we plowed into the deep snow in the median, doing a nearly complete 270 along the way. Now don't worry – we were fine, the car was fine, and a tow truck arrived in short order to get us out. But it was an inauspicious start to our family vacation.

And it didn't get better. When we arrived the next day, we found that the keys to the condo didn't work, the garage door wouldn't open, and our ski equipment didn't fit. The day after that, when everyone else arrived, my uncle's car wouldn't start, then my cousins were hit by a skidding car in a roundabout (they and their car are fine too), and the *other* car that my *other* cousin rented suddenly had all of its dashboard engine lights light up like a Christmas tree. Gathered around the family table that night, with three out of the five little kids sick and all of us adults exhausted, we all wondered if we shouldn't scrap the trip altogether. After all, it seemed like the next catastrophe would happen to one of us on the ski slopes. Even though I know intellectually that this isn't the way God works, I found myself thinking, "Maybe God is trying to tell us something. Maybe we should just go home!" After all, this trip was messy, everything was going wrong, and it almost felt like God wasn't with us at all.

Not much later, after the kids were put to bed, my cousin Susie and her husband Nick asked if I wanted to head out for a late-night snowshoe hike. Now you might be thinking, "That's the worst idea ever after all that's happened to you." I admit that I thought that too. But I decided to go anyway – you only live once right? And how often do I get to go snowshoeing with my cousins? The answer: exactly once in my whole life.

We headed off along a trail of packed snow into the mountains. The light of the moon guided our steps as we left civilization and climbed up through the trees. The air was still and cold; the world silent save for our breath and the flapping of the snowshoes; a planet shone brightly ahead of us – a beaming heavenly body for us to follow. We crossed a river that was mostly frozen, the gurgling of the water singing beneath the ice under our feet. Up and up we went, until we reached a clearing. Below us, the village of Vail was cupped in the valley; it's warm lights glowing between the shoulders of the mountains. Above us, the stars shimmered in the frigid night air, casting light on the snow that made it look as though someone had spilled a huge container of silver glitter on the sleeping world. The

Joy Thieves

branches of aspen trees, bare of leaves, were coated in a thin layer of ice, and when the moonlight caught them just right, it seemed as if a web of twinkling lights were suspended in the air around us. Standing there, a deep sense of wonder overtook me. The beauty and the silence, the vastness of the universe above and the grandeur of the mountains stretching to the sky around us – in these things there was something of the majesty and the mystery of God. There in the snow, in the middle of the mess of our vacation, the Spirit of Love drenched the world and filled me with the awe and the certainty that God was indeed *there*.

I wondered, then, if that's how the Wise Men felt when they finally finished that journey that brought them to Bethlehem. They had gone in search of a king; they were led to the most unlikely of birthplaces in the midst of a world that was a mess: imperial rule, subjugated people, poverty, injustice, crazy rulers like King Herod who were willing to kill small children. And they arrived at a house, came to a feeding trough, and found an ordinary mother and father holding an extraordinary child. There in the midst of the mess of the world, they came face to face with God – a manifestation of God that they could see and touch and hold – and I think they knew it. I think that awe and wonder and a sense of mystery washed over them in that moment and brought them to their knees to present their gifts.

And I'm not the only one who thinks that. On Epiphany – which we are observing today, though it is actually on January 6th – we celebrate God revealing God's own self to the Gentiles: to the Wise Men. We celebrate this as the day when those 'outsiders' recognized the love of God in the child of Jesus. Can you imagine what that would have felt like? Have you ever had a feeling like that – perhaps not so profound, but a feeling that God was somehow present with you, in a person, in an event, in nature?

The word epiphany means a manifestation of God – essentially, it means a moment when you know that, in the midst of everything, God has shown up. We celebrate *the* epiphany, *the* manifestation of God in Christ to the magi, but I think that many of us have had epiphany moments – moments like mine on that night in the mountains when in the middle of life's chaos and mess, the Lord is suddenly, breathtakingly present.

And according to Paul, we as the church – we as the Body of Christ in the world – we also have an epiphany call. In our Ephesians reading he says that, "through the church the wisdom of God in its rich variety may be made known to the rulers and authorities…" Paul says that it is the church that is responsible for making the wisdom of God known. No small task, right? Quite literally we might take this as a charge to go out and preach the gospel, which often brings to mind the kind of heavy handed evangelism that beats you over the head with guilt and sin in an effort to coerce you into belief – not something that we're generally comfortable with. But *I* hear in this something deeper, something subtler – I hear in this a wondrous and beautiful calling – I hear in this the call to be epiphany guides.

We all know that we cannot cause an epiphany to happen – that responsibility lies with God and God alone. It was God alone who appeared in the form of a child to the Wise Men. It was the Holy Spirit alone who opened me to the awe and divine mystery of that midnight hike. But the Wise Men wouldn't have gotten there without a star. I wouldn't have gotten there without my cousins. The truth is, sometimes we need help getting to the place where we can encounter the love of Christ. Sometimes we need a guide to lead us to that epiphany manifestation of God. And I think that we, as the church, are called to be those guides. Like the star, like my cousins, we are called to lead people to the places where they might have that epiphany moment. We don't force it to happen (how could we?), we probably don't even talk about God or Jesus or the Spirit at all, but we *do* guide the way, we are companions on the journey.

Sometimes that looks just like it did with Susie and Nick. Sometimes, in the midst of life's messes, we're called to walk with people to the places where *we've* encountered the love of God. That epiphany, that manifestation of Christ, may or may not happen, but we take the journey in reckless hope, trusting that God *wants* to show up.

But sometimes being an epiphany guide, well, it looks quite different. Sometimes we are epiphany guides simply by the way we live – simply by the way we love. By striving to act with a love that mirrors God's own – a love that is so deep and so wide that it accepts people as they are, where they are, yet holds onto the hope of who they *can* be at their most whole and healthy, a love that walks into the chaos of our world and stands steadfastly beside another – by striving to act with a love like that, perhaps the Lord can use even us to interrupt the mess of someone's life with the awe and wonder, the beauty and mystery of the presence of God. Perhaps the Lord can use even us to take someone's breath away with the strength of so great a love. Perhaps the Lord can use even us to breathe an epiphany to life.

Becoming a Pentecostal Church
Ezekiel 37:1-14; Acts 2:1-21

So a pastor and a medical marijuana dealer are sitting on a plane...

You're waiting for the punch line, aren't you? Because this does seem like the perfect setup for a joke. But it's not. This is what happened on one of my flights back home from Louisiana this past week. Now before I go on, you need to know something about some of us pastors: minus a few exceptions, we by and large do *not* like to talk to people on airplanes. It's not that we're rude or that we don't care or that we don't like conversations; it's just that quite often when it comes to plane rides you've got enough time for the person to ask what it is that you do for a living. And when you say, "I'm a minister," one of two things usually takes place: 1. You wind up becoming *their* minister for the duration of the flight, or 2. An awkward silence ensues followed by an awkward duration of the flight. This aversion to in-air conversation is so true for most of us that one of my colleagues at this past week's retreat confessed that she sometimes puts in her headphones even when she's not listening to anything just so her row-mates don't start talking.

So, there I was sitting in the exit row pulling out my ear buds, book in hand, when the guy sitting next to me says, "Are you heading home or away from home?" With an inward sigh I put the book in my lap and left my headphones in my purse, and I told him that I was headed home. Of course, the conversation didn't end there because somehow I had wound up sitting next to the chattiest person on the plane.

It was not long into the conversation that Tim – that was his name – shared with me that he was a medical marijuana grower and seller in Maine. He proceeded to show me pictures of his plants, tell me how much money he made (and that he hid it in the back yard instead of taking it to the bank), order a whiskey and sprite, and then pull out a clip of cash that had hundred dollar bills on the outside to pay for said drink. Now, I don't know what kind of preconceptions form in your mind when you hear and witness such details, but I can tell you what formed in mine. First, though I know many people find it helpful, I am honest enough to admit that I'm a bit hesitant when it comes to medical marijuana. So right off the bat I was thinking, *this is not the guy I want to be talking to.* Then there were the pictures and the drink order and the wad of cash, which only served to confirm and deepen my suspicion of him. I just generally found myself thinking that he and I lived in two very different worlds with very different goals in life – I found myself thinking that we spoke two very different languages.

And then Tim told me about his father. It wasn't too long ago that Tim's father died of cancer. He didn't tell Tim or Tim's siblings about his diagnosis until very late in the game – after the point when treatment would have been effective. Very quickly Tim's father was placed in hospice care. As he recounted this next part, Tim's voice grew noticeably thick with grief. "They had him on morphine and fentanyl," he said. "He was so doped up that he didn't really recognize that we were there, and he couldn't talk to us coherently at all. So I gave him some of my weed. And you know what? He was able to use that instead of the other drugs, and we were able to talk to him, to really be *with* him until the day that he died." Then Tim turned and looked me in the eyes and said with the kind of passion that spills over from the very heart of who we are, "I couldn't save his life, but I helped him have a good death – I helped him connect with me and my siblings. If I can truly help people to live fully by growing and selling pot, then I'll be happy. Because that's all that I really want – to help people. To give back."

It was then that I told him about what I do for a living. We made a crack about the pastor and the pot dealer who want to save the world sitting in the exit row. And then we started talking about the vision that we shared – the vision of a world made new, where suffering and poverty and hatred are at an end; where all people live full and healthy lives; where all children have access to education and safety; where our politicians work for the greater good and not the next election. Suddenly it was abundantly clear that we were speaking exactly the same language. Suddenly it was clear that we were in the midst of a Pentecostal moment – a fact I would not have recognized had it not been for my friend Emily.

See just the day before, on one of the only sunny days that we had while in Louisiana, Emily and I had braved the oppressive heat and dripping humidity to take a late-afternoon walk. Thinking about the week ahead, Emily declared that she loved Pentecost, and I looked at her as if she'd grown a second and then a third head. Pentecost is all well and good, but I can't say that I love it. So I found myself blurting out, "why?" And she said to me, "because the Spirit did an amazing thing that day – the Spirit allowed people who wouldn't ordinarily be able to even *understand* each other to communicate fluently so that they could join together in working for God."

I'd never thought about Pentecost that way before. But if you really sit back and think about what God was doing on that day, it's clear that Emily is right. Our scripture from Acts says that they were gathered together in one place when the Spirit came with the force of a violent wind and descended on each of the disciples. They began to speak about God in languages that none of them had ever studied before, and people from across the known world heard their words, heard about God's deeds of power and about Jesus the Christ and about the death of death itself. And do you know what happened next? Peter talks about this vision of what God through Christ was doing in the world. And the people wanted to join in that vision, so they repented and were baptized and became the group of followers known as the Church, working for the transformation of the world. *That* is what the Spirit was doing on Pentecost: moving through individuals to allow them to work with people who spoke completely different languages uniting them in the common purpose of working towards a world made new by the power of the resurrection. Uniting them in the common purpose of breathing life into the dry bones of strangers, friends and neighbors, just as Ezekiel did.

At our session meeting this past Wednesday night, Julie talked about all of the unrest in our world, and she said, "we need our own uprising." And she's right. We need our own uprising – an uprising that will bring peace, justice and love to *all* people, not just to some. She talked about this uprising coming from individuals coming together despite their differences to work towards the promise of God's Kingdom. In essence, we need an uprising of the Pentecostal church. Now I'm not talking about Pentecostal as a denomination;

I'm talking about *all* churches, *our* church – living into the promise of Pentecost. I'm talking about becoming a Pentecostal church that is made up of individuals who are open to hearing the words of the Spirit pouring forth from people we'd normally sneer at, people we'd normally dismiss as being from a different world, speaking a different language. I'm talking about putting down the headphones, the cell phone, the iPad; I'm talking about taking the time out of our busy days and long nights; I'm talking about looking for the face of Christ in every human being we meet – all so that we can be open to the conversations that lead us to a shared vision, that lead us to the kind of relationships where we can act together for the transformation of our hurting communities, our fractured cities, our divided country, and our war-torn world.

It seems unlikely that I'll ever see Tim again. He goes back and forth from Orlando to Maine; I, for the most part, stay in Baltimore. But you know how we ended that flight - by adding each other as friends on Facebook, by encouraging one another in our own, very different ministries. We ended the flight knowing that, as we went off into the world to work with the Spirit in bringing abundant life to all people, we weren't going off into the world alone. United by the Pentecostal Spirit, part of the Universal Pentecostal Church, we are a part of the world-wide uprising of the people of the resurrection, living into the call to bring transformation, healing and love to all.

Good Sheep
Just *before* the Baltimore uprising
Psalm 23; John 10:11-18

I was riding the bus home from school on that February day in 2002 when we all learned that Al Qaeda had beheaded Daniel Pearl. I don't know why I was on the bus that day – it was my senior year and I had long since started driving myself to school – but I remember clearly where we were on our route back to my house. And even more sharply defined in my memory is the way that I felt upon hearing the news: there was this sick sense of dread that washed down my throat and twisted my stomach, and my mouth went dry with anxiety. The gruesome violence of that murder hit me like an unexpected sucker punch to the gut. After watching the towers fall, it seemed like no act of violence by terrorists could surprise me, but this did.

Now, thirteen years later, I fear I've grown accustomed to hearing about the horrific violence perpetrated by groups spreading terror in the name of God. The mention of suicide bombers in the news, the kidnapping and murder of westerners, the militaristic attacks on public institutions – none of these seem to faze me anymore. I lament that they happen, I feel sorrow for the victims, but I am not filled with dread and anxiety. At least, I wasn't until the so-called Islamic State showed up on the scene. Their terrifying sweep through the Middle East – massacring minority ethnic groups, Christians, and even other Muslims who do not believe as they do – has revived the sense of fear that I felt in the months following 9/11 and Daniel Pearl's death. And from what I've heard from all of you, I'm not the only one who is afraid; I'm not the only one who is horrified and outraged. We're all asking the same question: what can we do? As disciples of Christ, as those who follow a loving God, what could we *possibly* do?

This week, stories of ISIS and stories of foreign terrorism and violence have taken a backseat to the news of Freddie Gray's death while in the custody of the Baltimore City Police Department – and rightfully so. There is much that is unknown about the case. What we do know is that the 25-year-old African American man was arrested on April 12th; while in the police van he told officers that he was having trouble breathing, but they did not immediately call for medical help. He was taken to Shock Trauma later, where it was discovered that his spinal cord was mostly severed. Freddie Gray died on April 19th – one week ago today. Throughout this week, protestors have filled the city streets, demanding justice for Mr. Gray and expressing the anger and fear of the African American community. The protests were peaceful, yet a spokesman for the Fraternal Order of Police referred to them as a "lynch mob." At our clergy retreat this week, one of our African American pastors expressed her outrage and sorrow at this statement; "he has no idea," she said. "My people have faced lynch mobs – he doesn't have any idea what that fear is like. You have no idea of the terror that we have to live with each day knowing that our sons might be killed by the very people who are sworn to protect us."

She's right. I have no idea. None at all.

I do know that opinions in this congregation have been divided when it comes to the recent deaths of black men at the hands of white police officers. But despite the differences in our thoughts about these cases, there is one thing that I hope we can all agree on: our African American neighbors across the country feel as though their lives are valued less highly than the lives of white Americans. These police cases have caused a geyser of feeling to erupt from emotions that were running just below the surface of our society. The African American community often feels marginalized, disenfranchised and stigmatized. Whether you believe that that is true or not, those feelings are a fact.

At this point you may be wondering what the death of Freddie Gray and the seemingly unstoppable force of ISIS have in common. You may be wondering why I jumped from the question of "what do we do about ISIS" to the events of this past week in Baltimore. It's because I believe that the two are inextricably linked.

Over the course of the last year, we've learned quite a bit about how groups like ISIS recruit. They look for young people who are feeling pushed to the margins, who are feeling disenfranchised by the society of which they are a part, and then they exploit those feelings. Terrorist groups give them a sense of purpose, make them feel included and valued – things they were not getting from their own community and country. And right now, right here in the United States, we have a lot of young men and women who are feeling unheard and under-valued; we have a lot of young men and women who are growing up in an adversarial culture where the very people whom they're supposed to look to for protection are seen rather as the agents of terror. That perception, whether right or wrong, is one that we have to take very seriously. Because the more that our young people feel like they're at the margins, the more they feel that they're deemed less valuable, less human because of the color of their skin or the religion that they practice or the people they fall in love with, the more likely they are to seek refuge in the arms of those who are experts in manipulating such emotions – experts who are likely to twist that negative self-image into hate.

So what are we to do? How do we, as Christians, respond to such a big, overwhelming problem? How do we work alongside our neighbors to bring healing to police and the communities they're supposed to serve? How do we combat the terrifying tidal wave of terrorist organizations like ISIS?

By being good sheep.

This week in the lectionary cycle is called "Good Shepherd Sunday." It's called that because we read the 23rd psalm and John 10, both of which are all about God as the Good Shepherd. And what does the Good Shepherd do? Three times in our gospel reading Jesus says some variant of, "The Good Shepherd lays down his life for his sheep." The Good Shepherd lays down his life. Of course, we understand that Jesus is talking about the crucifixion and resurrection. Our Good Shepherd – Christ – laid down his life in order that we might have life and have it abundantly. Our God laid down divinity in order to be born as a child, live as a man, die as a criminal and be raised to new life – all for us, for God's own sheep. And so what does that mean for us? What does it mean for us to be good sheep who follow the Good Shepherd?

According to the author of first John, it means that we are to follow Christ by laying down our lives for one another.

Now I know that that conjures up thoughts of martyrdom – of literally laying down our life for another person. But I don't think that's really what God has in mind for us – at least, not for most of us – especially in this day and age. So what *does* it mean to lay down our life for someone else? Think about the things you value most highly – the things you'd be loathe to give up. I don't mean physical things like a phone or the internet or your house; I mean things like time, your particular plans for how your future should go, or your expectations for someone else. When I hear these words from first John calling us to lay down our lives for one another, these things are the things I think of. I think of laying down what is important to me for the good of someone else – for instance, letting go of the aspirations that you were holding for how your child would turn out in order to let them pursue their own interests and passions, or giving up an opportunity to travel in order to be with a loved one going through health troubles, or carving out time in your busy schedule in order to be present for another human being.

And it's that last one, I think, that teaches us how to be good sheep when it comes to the big, big issues that we face in this day and age. Do we really want to feel like we're doing something to combat ISIS? Do we really care about our African American brothers and sisters – especially the young ones? Do we really want to combat the violence that is seeping through our inner city streets? Then let us be good sheep! Let us lay down our lives for our neighbors! Let us make the time to step out of what is comfortable in order that we might build healing relationships across racial, economic, and social boundaries.

It's going to take time – *our* time. And it's not going to be easy – there is a gaping hole where trust should be. But we have the power to join in the healing, reconciling work that the Spirit is already doing in our cities, our neighborhoods, our country. We have the power to be resurrection people simply by giving time to a stranger, by striking up a conversation with someone whom we'd normally walk right by, by building relationships with the people who walk down our streets each day. It's going to take time, and it's not going to be easy, but this is where the work of reconciliation begins. This is where the power of the resurrection calls us. This is where we begin to combat the violence and hatred of this world and, in doing so, find that it is not just healing for the other, but it is also healing for us – *we* are made more whole, more joyous, more abundantly alive.

Lydia
Acts 16:9-21; Revelation 21:10, 21:22-22:5

(Turned away from the congregation) Welcome to Lydia's purple cloth emporium, give me just one moment and I'll be right with you! (turning around) Oh! Forgive me – but…you all aren't Roman, are you? Where are you from? Right, of course, how could I have forgotten – you're the American group aren't you? Is it true; are you really all *Christians*? And you meet together in a building that's openly dedicated to worshiping Jesus as the Christ? I can't even imagine that – how wonderful it must be for you! And you must have such an impact on your community being so visible! I'm so excited that you're here!

But of course, I'm getting ahead of myself. My name is Lydia, and I understand that you're here to learn more about my story? I'm a much older woman now, but I'm happy to tell you what I can – what I remember of it. I have to say, it's still hard to believe that it got written down – and put into a whole new set of scriptures! It absolutely boggles my mind to think you all are still reading about me – of course, a much younger me! And I guess that's where the confusion comes in because with all of the years between me and you – well, your life must be very different from mine. And I could understand that that would leave many of you with a lot of questions. So here I am to try to clear things up – as much as I can anyway.

As you already know, I'm from the city of Thyatira in Macedonia, and I deal in purple cloth. Oh, not so much me anymore – my sister's grandchildren do most of the work. There's good money in this business, always has been – cloth like this is considered a luxury around here, so one can get a pretty penny for it. And yes, I *was* and am an unmarried woman, the head of my household I suppose you could say. Which isn't the easiest way to go in this part of the empire in this particular day and age. I do all right for myself, though. But then, I suppose you've heard the rumors: that I'm actually very well off and enjoy high social standing here in the city. I won't admit that that's true – but I'm not going to deny it either. Let's just say, when it comes to standing up to the Roman Empire – I've always had something to lose. And keep that in mind, because that matters.

But even though I *have* something to lose, I can't say that I'm particularly *pro*-Rome. Because I've seen enough to know that there are ways in which the Empire is like one big bully. They use violence and overwhelming military power to get what they want – but I suppose you know that already. And that wasn't really what got to me in the end. It was something in the culture – the drive for prosperity, the injustice in the system – no one watched out for those who were vulnerable. When I was a much younger woman – long before I ever met Paul or any of the other Christians – I was walking home after running an errand for my parents, and I passed this girl in the street. She was my age, but her face was bruised and dirty. I almost didn't recognize her; in fact, I passed her by before I looked back and realized that we had been friends once when we were little. And it hit me – I remembered my parents talking one night about how her family had fallen into debt. It wasn't uncommon in those days for a family like hers to sell their children into slavery as payment. But to see it…that was a different thing altogether. Because she and I were not so different. Our families were not so different. If my parents had been just a little bit less lucky or if we hadn't been able to produce such fine purple cloth, that could have been me. That could have been me. I remember feeling sick when I realized that. Sick and so very angry that something like that could happen in the grandest empire in the world. Have you ever seen something like that – seen something that was just unfair, not right – *dehumanizing?* But what could *I* do? I was just a little Macedonian girl. I'll never forget it, though. I'll never forget it.

I guess that's why I became what we called at the time 'a worshiper of God.' That meant that I followed the Jewish way of life – believed in their God – even though I wasn't actually an Israelite. See, most people here in the empire worship the whole pantheon of gods. And occasionally, we'll even get an emperor who thinks we should worship him as a deity too (cra*zy*). But not the Israelites. Even after they were conquered – by the Babylonians, the Greeks, the Romans – they kept their own religion. I always thought that they were so brave to do such a thing. Because like I said, the Romans are capable of being brutal; all that they really care about is preserving and expanding their empire and their power. So it's alright for a group like the Israelites to practice their own religion as long as it keeps the peace. But the minute a local leader thinks that it's causing some sort of insurrection or instability in the region – the minute it becomes a threat – then trust me; the Romans will squash you like a bug. And a bug trying to cross the main road into Rome on a parade day would have better odds of surviving than you would. You can take my word for that. But the Israelites, they kept their religion anyway. Even after Jews in Jerusalem tried to take back their city and the temple was destroyed and so many were killed and so many others were scattered, *still* they kept on worshipping their one God. Such crazy bravery. Standing up to the Roman bully – it drew me in. But in all honesty, as much as I loved God, I don't think that I would have given my life to stand up to Rome. What would it have accomplished? It wasn't like we God worshipers were going to change the Empire. We just had to wait the empire out.

That's the way that I felt back then. That's the way a lot of us felt back then. We kept our heads down, helped those we could with money or food, worked hard, worshiped. And then one day, one Sabbath, I was sitting with some women just outside of the city by the river when these men showed up. And they started talking about this rabbi named Jesus. They said that he was *God* but that he had taken on our human-ness in order to help us break free from all of the powers in this world that sought to keep us from fully living. At first, we thought they were crazy – I suppose you must be used to hearing that Christ was God made human. But to us, that was about as nuts as saying the Emperor was a god. But the more Paul talked, the more we heard the passion and power in his voice. It was like he himself had been transformed – like he himself had experienced this Jesus' power and had been set free from all of the darkness in his own life that tried to hold him back from living fully. And he told us that Jesus was killed by Rome but that death couldn't hold him and he'd risen again. All over the Empire, he said, people were hearing this same story and believing – they were completely changing the way that they lived. They were setting captives free and standing up for those who couldn't stand up for themselves. We witnessed it for ourselves the very next day – there was this slave-girl who was being exploited by her owners because of her ability to tell fortunes. Paul saw how she was being used and commanded that the spirit holding her hostage come out. And she was free – it made her owners very angry, but she was fully herself again, fully human – and they couldn't exploit her anymore. I couldn't help but think of my friend – and how badly I wanted to change things for her. Suddenly, I felt this hope, this excitement, this passion beginning to burn within me. Because if God had come and broken free of death, and if God was sending the Spirit to each one of us, then God was giving us the power to actually stand up to Rome like Paul stood up to the slave owners – God was giving us the power to actually make a *difference*, a real difference. I was giddy and excited and more hopeful than I had ever been in my life. They came and baptized my family that day. And you know what – for the first time I think I felt the power of God dwelling within me. It was this sense that *I* was powerful – that *I* could make a difference. So I invited Paul and those with him to stay with me.

To someone on the outside, that would have seemed a crazy, stupid thing to do. Because these men, like Jesus before them, they were seen as disrupters of the peace and therefore liable to be held accountable by Roman justice. And I let them into my home! I was basically waving a banner of support! I could have lost everything – and remember, I had a lot to lose! But here's the thing – I couldn't have done otherwise. See, up until I was baptized, religion was just something I believed. But hearing about Jesus, knowing that there was this Spirit of power within me and that God was working to transform the world – it demanded that I *act*. That was part of being a Christ-follower – we didn't just *believe*, we *lived* our beliefs in a countercultural way. We stood up to bullies and stood with the poor and the widows and the orphans. We stood with the outcasts. And we did it because that's what God was doing in the world and we were called to join in.

Of course, we were also human. After Paul left, we started meeting together, to talk about Christ and God and what the Spirit was up to in the world – how the Spirit was transforming us and the people around us. We pooled our resources and we broke bread. But eventually some of that initial passion wore off and after a few years, coming together for worship became more about us and less about God – we stopped asking where God was calling us to go next and were content just to be together once a week. We got caught up in our work and our family lives and it was easy to forget that we were supposed to be living out this faith – standing up to the powers of injustice in this world. I know I was no exception – my business thrived because the rich got richer at the expense of the poor. And it was easy to turn a blind eye to it so that I could stay comfortable. It was easy to keep quiet to stay safe.

That's why that man, John of Patmos, wrote his whole apocalypse. He saw how the churches were losing their passion, how they were failing to be countercultural and stand up to the tyranny of Rome. And he called them out on it. He painted this picture of Christ at war with a horrific beast that rose up out of the waters – that beast was the Roman Empire. He wanted us to see how Rome was taking God's place by using violence to claim ultimate power and demanding that we all worship the Emperor as a god. And at the end, he paints this beautiful picture of how God's city is supposed to look – open to all the nations, lit by the light of God, with a tree that grows for the healing of all peoples. The holy city – Christ's city – where they need no light, nor lamp, nor sun because Christ is their all. We needed to see that, to remember what we were working towards. What *God* had been working towards from the very beginning, what God had given us the power to help bring about.

It was a *big* vision – and a very long way off from where we were. But that vision, it reminded us that we had a role to play in this world. It reminded us that we had to *live* our beliefs like we did in the beginning. And so we started asking ourselves – would anyone notice if our congregation disappeared? Would our community care if we suddenly ceased to be there? In the beginning, we were sad to say the answer was no. Maybe some of the poor would notice that we stopped providing them with money, but we had stopped living our faith in a way that made a difference.

It took time – time spent in prayer to get in touch with the Spirit within, time spent remembering those powerful stories of where we had seen God transform people and communities, time spent listening to how Christ was calling us to act now, time spent remembering the anger at the injustice that we had seen – the anger that gave us reason to act. It took time, but we got our passion back; we got our living faith back. Still, we never stop asking – would our community care if our congregation disappeared? Would anyone notice?

Life is a Highway
Isaiah 35:1-10

My second year of university, before my mom moved to the Midwest, she and I drove the 3,000 miles from our home in Philadelphia to my school near San Francisco. It was the first year that we attempted driving, so we didn't quite have the route worked out, and one day we found ourselves on a two-lane highway that stretched on seemingly forever in front of us as it wound through the deserts of Nevada. That was my first experience in such desolate terrain and it was more than a little bit frightening. Miles and miles passed and we saw no one and nothing except vast expanses of hot sand and rocky earth that supported little vegetation and less wildlife. Even our windscreen was remarkably free from the insects that usually splattered there. Mobile reception was spotty at best—if the car broke down it was impossible to say how far we would have to walk before finding a speck of civilization in that barren place or another motorist willing to help us. And in the blazing heat, with the air conditioner blasting, the arid air that circulated through the car sucked the moisture from our eyes and lips making them painfully dry, and the simple act of drawing it into our lungs with each breath made us thirsty. It didn't take long before I was at the point of wanting to be out of the desert and be out of it *now*.

A couple of days ago, the song "Life is a Highway" by Tom Cochrane got stuck in my head—if you don't know it, the name pretty much says it all. But if Mr. Cochrane is right, and life *is* a highway, then I think it's pretty safe to say that sooner or later we all find ourselves on a stretch of desolate desert road, like my mom and I did, wanting to be out and out *now*.

The circumstances that create such barren wastelands in the midst of our journeys are different for each of us—perhaps it's a physical infirmity or a mental one, like depression or anxiety; perhaps it's a loss, of someone you love, or a position that you've held for years, or of financial stability; or perhaps it's a broken relationship, a family fractured by fighting, a trust that's been betrayed one time too many. Whatever the particularity that lands us in the desert, if we think for a moment over our lives we can all identify those times when we look around and all that we can see for miles is an endless stretch of road winding through sun and sand. We keep walking, keep living our lives, but there is a certain hollowness to it—somewhere deep down is the knowledge that this arid air has sucked something out of us and we aren't *truly* alive, at least not in the way that Jesus meant when he said that he came that we might have life and have it abundantly. And in the midst of the desert, it's hard to see how we're ever going to get to the other side. Sometimes, the wind is so strong that sand gets blown over the road such that we cannot even see it anymore and we are lost entirely.

Of course, this is not at all a *new* phenomenon. The highway of life has been leading people and nations alike into the desert for as long as there has been a written history to record it. The Israelites were certainly no different. When our passage from Isaiah was written they were a people in exile—driven away from their homes and into foreign lands. Overcome by an empire much larger and much more powerful than they had ever been, there didn't seem to be any hope that they would ever be reestablished as a nation. They had always understood themselves to be a people chosen by God, held and protected by the Lord who had made a covenant with them centuries before; I cannot even begin to imagine how that period of exile must have fundamentally shaken their sense of identity and how very, very difficult it must have been to trust that God's promises of restoration would ever come to pass. The people were *alive*, but they weren't really *living*, at least, not as the great nation that the Lord said they would be when God spoke to Abraham so many years before.

And into this lifeless waste, Isaiah spoke: "the desert will rejoice, and flowers will bloom in the wilderness. The desert will sing and shout for joy; it will be as beautiful as the Lebanon Mountains and as fertile as the fields of Carmel and Sharon. Everyone will see the Lord's splendor, see his greatness and power." They are words of great hope indeed, but it's not hard for me to imagine the people looking at one another in disbelief and some brave soul tugging at Isaiah's robe, saying, "great speech, but we're in *exile*. We don't want the desert to bloom, we want a way *out!*" It is, in fact, curious that God's promise to the people should start here—with the barren wilderness turning into fertile paradise—as opposed to with the highway that will lead them back to Jerusalem. It begs the question: why? Why should the Lord begin with a transformation of the desert instead of the Road of Holiness that leads *home*? What's the point in turning the burning sands into crystal cool lakes and the dry land into bubbling springs if the people are just going to move on anyway?

Perhaps it's just a figure of speech, a poetic device that the prophet uses to express the incredible joy that the people will experience as they return to their homeland. This passage *is* an incredible piece of poetry; after all, it wouldn't be all that far-fetched to think such a thing.

Perhaps…but I believe that Isaiah is pointing to a deeper truth here, one that speaks to the deserts of our lives as much as it did to the desert of exile that the Israelites experienced.

I often hear people say, in the midst of those long stretches when life seems barren, that everything happens for a reason. I'm not sure that I agree, at least, not entirely. See, the subtle implication inherent in the statement is that someone—namely, God—*caused* the event to happen in order to bring about a specific result. And while I don't pretend to understand the mysteries of the Almighty, it is very hard for me to believe that a Lord who loves us enough to take on our humanity would also author the tragedies that befall us in life. Instead, I believe that the God of our salvation can *redeem* every situation, no matter how terrible. And *this*, I think, is what Isaiah is talking about when he writes of the blossoming of the desert, the dry ground growing fertile and springs of water flooding up from arid earth. It is the poetic expression of God's power to transform a situation that was life-draining into one that is life-*giving*.

When Jesus was born, the Israelites were still a subjugated people, returned to their homeland, yes, but living under a succession of oppressors from the Persians to the Greeks to the Romans. That desert period in the life of the nation that was so vividly apparent in the time of the exile hadn't really come to an end—the people were still languishing, they were still looking for a way *out*, waiting for the Messiah that would reestablish them as a mighty kingdom, as a light to the nations. They had found the road *home* but the gaping wound of defeat remained. And the effects of this unhealed wound bled through the Israelite society, draining life from the people as a dry wind sucks moisture from all that it touches. Sects formed within the community as people tried to cope with their circumstances. The Zealots fought for freedom, using what we might now call terrorist tactics against the Romans and their own countrymen who collaborated with them. The Pharisees attempted to reclaim their identity as a holy people through a more stringent adherence to the law, in some cases losing sight of the grace of God, which was at its heart. Conflict and hardship persisted; oh the exile was over, but somehow they weren't out of the desert.

And if we are honest with ourselves, the same is true of our own lives. We do our very best to claw our way out of the barren stretches—we have no desire to wait patiently for God to change the landscape into something livable, so we find other ways to cope with our pain, our anger, our shame, and we try to pretend that whatever it was that created the desert in the first place is over and done with, in the past, long left in the rearview mirror. We're fine, we tell people, trying to convince ourselves as much as them that it's true. The problem with this is that somehow, eventually, the unhealed wounds of our lives find their way to the surface in sometimes unexpected ways. Anger at God and life over an illness that left us permanently disabled comes out as anger toward the ones we love. Heartache over a broken family twists into a bitter despair that can only be numbed by endless hours of work or TV or something even stronger. The shame of losing a job slowly chips away at our self-esteem until we begin to think that we truly are worthless and stop trying to accomplish anything at all. The event may be long past, but the life-draining conditions remain. And when we are living in darkness ourselves, it is next to impossible to be a light to others.

And so we return to the question of "why?" Why the transformation of the desert before the road home? Isaiah describes God changing terrain that cannot support life into fertile ground that is ideal for growth…and *this*, I think, is what God is doing in redeeming the tragedies, the failures, the losses of our lives—healing our wounds such that they can give life not only to *us*, but to those around us as well. We cannot truly walk on that Road of Holiness, singing and shouting for joy, authentically proclaiming the good news of the Lord if our souls are being sucked dry by unhealed scars. It is when we witness our own desert bursting forth into bloom by the power of God's Spirit, bearing fruit in ways that we never imagined possible, that the song of rejoicing becomes robust, drawing others into the light and shining as a beacon of hope to those yet languishing.

Years ago I met a man whose life rang out with just such a song of joy. There was nothing overly dramatic about him; he wasn't anyone particularly special. A psychiatrist by profession, he worked with children and young adults struggling with depression, anxiety and other mental illnesses and by all accounts he was very good at it. At one point I asked him what it was that made him so successful. "When I was younger," he said, "I, myself, suffered with depression. It was one of the most difficult periods of my life. I was hopeless and angry and honestly didn't believe that there was a brighter future for me. Even when I did eventually get better, I was still ashamed of what I'd been through; I thought that I was a failure for having been sick and was terrified that someone might find out and condemn me for it. But then I went to medical school and discovered something entirely different. I *know* what it's like to be in my patients' shoes, to be suffering with a mental illness. When I say that things can get better, I know that it's true from my own experience. For the most part, my patients will never know my history, but I can connect with them on a deeper level because of it. The illness that I was so ashamed of has turned out to be one of the greatest assets I have. My success, I suppose, comes from the fact that I've lived through it." God transformed this man's desert into fertile ground, redeeming life draining illness such that it became life-giving.

We talk about advent being a season of waiting—of waiting for Christ to come and ransom captive Israel. We remember the words of the prophets, that the people walking in darkness would see a great light, that the year of the Lord's favor was coming. We sing of how the Christ child was born to set the people free—to heal their wounds that they might be light and salt to a world in need. We tell the story of star and angel, of the coming of the Messiah who would cause springs of living water to well up in the dry souls that were dying of thirst.

Joy Thieves

But advent is not just a time of looking back, of expectation for an event that happened 2,000 years ago, nor is it an event that ends on December 25th, not to return again until the following year. Each time the highway of life swerves into desert land, we enter into advent anew, waiting patiently for the coming of Christ, for the healing touch of our Savior and Lord who can transform even our most desolate of times into rivers flowing with living water. Standing in the middle of an endless expanse of sand and sun, we wait with hopeful expectation for the advent of the one who turns *our* burning earth into a lake and causes the flowers to bloom in *our* wilderness and makes *our* dry land sing and shout for joy! Strengthen your hearts, beloved, for the coming of the Lord is near!

So Stay Here Until…
Luke 24:36b-48 (and 49)

This past Monday morning started off with something of a mystery – a minor one to be sure, but a mystery nonetheless. If you have a Bible in front of you, I'm going to invite you to open it to Luke 24 – that's where all of this started earlier this week. I was sitting down with our morning prayer group and we turned to the reading assigned for this morning: Luke 24 from the second half of verse 36 to verse 48. Without even reading the passage, does anyone notice anything odd about those assigned verses – 36 to 48? What struck me before I ever skimmed over the content of the story was that the people who created the lectionary decided to leave off the last verse of the paragraph: verse 49. It's not *technically* a part of the reading for today. But why? It seems innocuous enough: "And see, I am sending upon you what my Father promised; so stay here in the city until you have been clothed with power from on high." Why omit it?

It's striking, isn't it, how similar the beginning of this passage is to the passage that we read last week from the Gospel of John? The disciples are together in a room, and Jesus appears among them saying, "Peace be with you!" He shows them his wounds, he commissions them to be witnesses. Yes, there is a lot that is similar to John 20. Except in John's account Jesus says, "As the Father has sent me, so I send you." John's Jesus sends the disciples out into the world to spread the good news of the resurrection. And what does Jesus say in Luke's account? "So stay here in the city until you have been clothed with power from on high." You know, in all my years of being in church, in four years of seminary, I cannot remember anyone ever talking about how bizarre these words from Jesus are. And they *are* bizarre – because in this respect, Luke's account of Christ's actions after the resurrection is different from all of the other Gospels. We've already mentioned John – there Jesus commands the disciples to go out. The same is true of Matthew where Jesus gives the disciples the great commission to go and baptize all nations. In Mark, Jesus sends his followers into the world from east to west to proclaim the good news. Matthew, Mark and John agree: Christ sends the disciples *out*.

But not Luke. In Luke's account, Jesus says to his disciples: *stay here*. And that's not all. In the story just before our passage for today – the walk to Emmaus – Jesus appears to two of his followers who are *leaving* the city of Jerusalem, causing them to *go back* to where the rest of the disciples are. While all the other Gospels are moving Christ's followers out into the world, Luke is calling them back to the city where the crucifixion happened. He's calling them together and telling them to remain where they are. It's not for an indefinite period of time – just until they are clothed with power from on high, which happens on Pentecost – but let's be honest, that's still fifty days away for these people. *Fifty* days! Fifty days of staying in the city and waiting.

It makes sense to me that some church leaders might not want to include this verse in the lectionary for today. After all, with so much anxiety in our denomination about Presbyterian decline, with so much energy being put into pushing our congregations *out* of their comfort zones, *out* of their walls, *out* into the world, an injunction from Christ to "stay here" seems like the last thing you'd want people to hear, right? This seems like a dangerous thing for Jesus to say. So why this command to "stay here until…?"

Last weekend I was down on the Eastern Shore, and when I'm there I don't have the usual amenities of high-tech society. I can't stream Netflix, there's no cable, no DVR, so I'm stuck watching the DVDs that I bring with me. Well, I decided to go back to a high school favorite: Gilmore Girls. In the first season, Rory – a young high school student – starts going out with her first boyfriend. They make it through three months, and then the boyfriend dumps her. Of course, Rory is crushed. Her mom tells her she should stay in her pajamas all day and eat ice cream and wallow. But Rory doesn't want to be the kind of girl who lets the end of relationship bring her down, so she instead throws herself into busy-work: running errands with her mom, reading for school, even going to a party she has no real interest in attending. Of course, she can't keep it up – she can't run from her emotions forever, so by the end of the episode what does she do? She wallows.

Now most of us gathered here this morning are quite a bit beyond our first breakup of youth. But many of us as individuals – and all of us as a congregation – are in a season of transition in our lives. As a congregation we've accepted a new sense of call, and we're beginning to take steps to live into it. As individuals, some of us are changing careers or retiring, some of us are feeling shifts in our relationships with friends or significant others, some of us are facing the realities of life after the diagnosis of an illness, and some of us are realizing that we need to let go of expectations that we had for how our lives or our work or our families would turn out. And since change in life is inevitable, even if this isn't where you are *right now*, it's likely where you will be in the not-too-distant future. And here's my question: how many of us have taken the advice that Rory's mom gave her – how many of us have set aside time to wallow? And I don't mean that in the "sit in self-pity eating ice cream and watching sappy movies" kind of way that many of us might think of when we hear the word. What I mean is: how many of us have given ourselves the space to acknowledge what we're leaving behind? Because no matter what the transition is, no matter how healthy or positive or exciting it may be, change always involves some degree of loss. In fact, from our Christian perspective, we might look at these transitions as opportunities for the power of the resurrection to be at work within us, as they offer us the possibility of growing into the fuller, more abundant life that Christ promises. But that means that these transitions also carry something of Good Friday with them – for there is no Easter without the tomb.

We are called to be resurrection people. We are called to be people who look for and point to that new life taking shape within us and around us. But I think there are times when we each wonder how, exactly, we're supposed to do that. And I think the answer lies in Jesus' command to the disciples to "stay here until."

Imagine yourselves in the position of that first group of Christ's followers for a moment. It's Easter Sunday, but Jesus hasn't appeared among you yet. What are you feeling? Pain, anger, doubt, sadness, guilt, fear – all of these are possible. Then Jesus appears and there's a surge of relief, of wonder, of hope, perhaps with some more doubt and fear mixed in. But what about after all of that? Jesus gives the disciples a mission – to be witnesses to the resurrection – and he tells them that they will be equipped for that mission. But then Christ leaves *again*. He disappears and then later ascends into heaven. So what are you, the disciples, feeling *now*? If I imagine myself in their place, I find that I would still be feeling a lot of sorrow, a lot of sadness – and perhaps even some anger. Yes, this spectacular miracle has happened. Yes, Jesus is the Messiah that we expected. Yes, the bonds of death have been broken. But this friend that I've been following for these last few years is still *gone*. I no longer have him beside me, teaching me, supporting me day in and day out. And on top of losing him, I'm soon going to be losing the way of life that I've become accustomed to. Instead of being a disciple, learning and following, I'll soon be an apostle – teaching, witnessing, and working with the Spirit for the healing and liberation of the world. The familiarity of my life for the last few years will soon disappear as this strange, wonderful, terrifying new journey begins.

And Jesus knows all of this, and in his infinite grace Jesus says, "stay here until…" Stay here until the Spirit comes. Stay here for the next fifty days and give yourself time and space to acknowledge, honor and grieve what you're losing as you grow into this new and abundant life. For Christ, the wounds of Good Friday have already healed – he is risen! For the disciples, the wounds that they suffered on Good Friday are still in the process of healing – but with time, they will be risen too.

And therein lies the wisdom of this tiny omitted verse from the Gospel of Luke. To be truly people of the resurrection – to be truly people who notice the new and abundant life blossoming within us and around us – we cannot rush past the tombs of Good Friday. When it comes to transitions in our lives – even if it is the most exciting job promotion or the happiest proposal or the most welcome chance to move – we need to hear the voice of Christ whispering to us: stay here until. Stay here in this place of transition until you've acknowledged, honored and perhaps even grieved what it is that you're leaving behind. Stay here – don't rush ahead, don't try to be superhuman, don't try not to feel – but stay here, pause here, give yourself space here to be honest about what you're leaving behind. Stay here until the wounds of the tomb are healed and you are risen indeed!

Grave Patience
John 11:17-44; Psalm 30

Awareness comes slowly, like waking from an exhausted sleep. There were no dreams, no moments of fitful half-slumber, no movements toward premature rousing, there was just lacking – a lack of consciousness, a lack of thought, even a lack of being. There was nothing, or so it seemed, until this unfolding moment of returning awareness and even it is achingly slow.

The first thing that registers is the dark. Though he thinks his eyes are open it is impossible to tell; there is no light to guide him, no light to let him know that he hasn't gone blind, no light to reassure him that his sight, like his awareness, will return even if it happens slowly. It is dark and it is cold – a damp kind of cold that radiates from the packed earth beneath him and clings to his skin with an ominous sort of clamminess. His first instinct, blind as he appears to be, is to put his hands out to the side and feel the ground to get some bearing on where he could possibly be – but his hands don't move. They are bound to one another as if they were one appendage; and a quick pull on his feet reveals a similar state of immobility. With awareness comes the first twinge of fear, the first pang of anxiety.

It is the silence and the smell that move him towards full-blown panic. There are no sounds save the steady but rapidly quickening tempo of breath filling his lungs and then leaving them, his pulse pounding in his ears. But the smell is overpowering – it is the stench of the dead colored with the last lingering hints of fragrance from the burial balms and spices – frankincense, myrrh. He doesn't need to see to know that he is in the presence of death, of decline, of decay. He doesn't need to see to know that he is likely in a tomb hewn of rock, in a sealed grave, buried alive. It is this knowledge that brings panic, edging out any memory of how he came to be here or any rational thought as to what might happen next. It is this knowledge that brings panic because the danger is clear. He's not dead right now, but he could be soon if he doesn't find a way out of this place.

He takes deep breaths, trying to ignore the smell of rot. For a moment he is paralyzed by fear, and he closes his eyes and tries to push reality away, tries to convince himself that this is just a dream, and if he could just go back to sleep, he'd wake and see that none of it was real. But he cannot convince himself and so he thrashes to his feet, staggering awkwardly from side to side with no particular direction or coherence. He bumps into walls and stumbles over small rocks and changes course when he meets resistance without any guiding principle except that he does not want to die in this tomb and must therefore get out. These are Lazarus' first moments of resurrection, at least as I imagine them.

The truth is, John doesn't tell us very much about what the whole being-raised-from-the-dead experience was like from Lazarus's perspective inside the tomb. For the most part, the dead man is a passive character who appears alive at just the right moment to stun the crowd, causing some to believe in Jesus as Lord and striking fear into the hearts of others. But I've always wondered what it was like for Lazarus, on the receiving end of that great gift of life. I've always wondered what was happening behind that boulder as Christ spoke to the crowd and prayed to God. I've always wondered if Lazarus had an experience of trying to deny that he was in a tomb or looking for his own way out like the account I just shared with you – it was mostly an academic sort of wondering, at least until a few weeks ago. A few weeks ago, though, in a time of my own anxiety, that wondering became personal.

It was early Wednesday morning, and I found myself driving to the emergency veterinary clinic with my beloved dog, Cyrus, dazed and droopy on the backseat of my car. Just a day earlier he had been running and jumping – all around his normal energetic self. But very suddenly I found that I had a very sick dog. Over the course of the next few days, I watched as he declined until late on Friday night when the vet called to say that the time had come to discuss euthanasia.

I experienced more grief and anxiety in those days than I imagined that I would when it came to this point in Cyrus' life. I did not expect there to be the waves of sorrow that crashed over me and then receded only to crash over me again. He's a dog, after all, and an old one at that – thirteen years old. Thirteen happy, and, until now, healthy years old. But I do not believe that it was his impending death alone that was causing my pain. As I reflected on our lives together, I realized that something deeper was going on. In the 12 years since I had adopted Cy, we had moved from death towards new life together. I was in high school when I got him – it was just after my dad left our family. Cyrus' family had walked out on him. We were both a mess. He chased after cars in a terrifying display of self-destruction. I had my own self-destructive tendencies. He lashed out; I lashed out. But over the years we both changed – we both grew profoundly in our capacity to trust and to love. We both settled. It seemed like our days in the tomb might finally be coming to an end. And so when I faced this moment of saying goodbye, it *was* a goodbye to an incredible friend whom I deeply loved. But it was also in a way a goodbye to a piece of my very self – I was saying goodbye to this wonderful creature who had walked with me through the very darkest of my days and who had stood faithfully by me while we waited for the stone to be rolled back and for new life to begin. And now, still surrounded by rocky walls but walking towards the fresh air it seemed like Cyrus' journey might head in a different direction than mine, and I found I wasn't ready to let go of the familiarity of life as it had been. I was afraid and uncertain. I grieved.

During those days I reacted to the fear by alternately trying to stick my head in the sand so that I wouldn't have to face the reality of the situation and then racing to and fro looking for any way to get out of the tomb other than what appeared to be the inevitable. The story of Lazarus started echoing in my head, and I began to wonder – could this be what he felt like before he heard Jesus' voice? Could this be what he experienced when he first came to awareness and realized he was sealed in a tomb?

It is not unreasonable to believe that the answer is yes. Think of the last time you experienced the fear and anxiety that comes when you realize that the world around you is changing such that you too must change or risk being left behind…but you aren't sure *how* to change. Think of those times when it became apparent that your life was taking a dramatic turn, and you were going to have to let go of what was familiar and head out in a new direction – but you didn't yet

Joy Thieves

know what that direction was. Think of those times when you found yourself in a tomb, but you didn't yet know how the stone was going to be rolled back. Perhaps it's because you lost your job. Perhaps it's because you lost a loved one. Perhaps it's because you decided to walk away from something – a career, a habit, a person – who was draining the life out of you and you wanted to be fully alive. Think about those times and think about how you reacted to them. The temptation is to do one of two things, I think: to try to ignore the reality of the situation – to try to blind yourself to the fact that you're in a tomb; or to try frantically to make your own way out – hacking at the walls, burrowing through the floor, blasting away at the stone. It's a flurry of activity for activity's sake, because we need to be doing *something* to get out of here.

The truth is, we even run into this temptation here in our lives together at church. Friends, we know that we're at a turning point. We know that we are, in a way, sitting in a tomb. We are not dead – we see the spark of new life in worship, in morning prayer and bible study, we see it in welcoming new members and in baptisms; we see it in our mission partnerships and in our youth. But we're not fully resurrected yet. We haven't quite *left* these stone walls. And this is a scary, anxiety-filled placed to be. Because we can't help but wonder – what if we *don't* make it out? What if we die here? And so it's tempting to try to ignore the brutal facts – that we *are* still entombed – and focus *only* on the positives. And it's just as tempting to start looking for our own way out of this place.

But the gospel offers us another option, a *better* option. After Lazarus bumbled his way around the cave for a while, he must have heard the stone being rolled back. And he must have stopped and listened long enough to hear Christ's voice saying, "Lazarus, come out!" The voice of a dear friend – the voice of his Lord – it gave him something to follow when he couldn't see anything at all. It gave him the hope of new direction. It was a lifeline leading him out of the tomb and back to the land of living. The promise of the gospel is that, just as Christ called to Lazarus, so Christ calls to us, showing us the direction in which we should head even if we can't see the destination; giving *us* a lifeline to the land of the living. The promise is that God is working even in our darkest night to turn our weeping into joy. The promise is that the Spirit is ever moving to turn our mourning into dancing. But we, like Lazarus, must get our heads out of the sand long enough, we must stop our hurried activity long enough, to hear Christ's call, to sense God working, to feel the Spirit moving. We must be patient in our grief, in our anxiety, in our fear – in all of those moments when we least feel like we are able to be patient – that we might truly hear our Lord calling us out of the grave and into new and abundant life.

And we must be patient for the long haul, because resurrection takes time. Consider the words of the Psalmist who said that weeping may linger for the night, but joy comes with the morning. It's such a deceptive line of poetry, making it sound for all the world like sorrow is turned off like a light switch when the sun breaks free of the horizon. But this Psalmist was one who knew pain – this was someone who had come close to death, either literally or figuratively, and had been revived once more. Most of us know well that recovery from illness, from suffering, from grief is a process – it takes a lot of time. And I think this Psalmist knew that too. The Hebrew word for linger in this verse literally means "to spend the night" or "to be a lodger for the night". And we all know well that houseguests don't just up and disappear. They take time to gather their belongings, to pack, to eat. As the sky turns gradually from black to gray until the rosy light of the sun finally touches the clouds, the houseguest gradually gets herself together to go home. The one recedes as the other gradually takes its place. And so it is with our sorrow turning to joy. So it is with our journey out of the tomb. It is a gradual change.

When we think of the resurrection – whether it be Christ's or Lazarus' – we think of that startling moment when they walk out of the tomb, vibrant and full of life. But God was surely working in those days that led up to that moment, in those days of entombment. The Spirit was surely in those graves, breathing life into the still, cold air of death. Resurrection, both for Christ and for Lazarus, took time. Resurrection for us takes time. If we truly desire to walk out of these tombs – to make our way back to the land of the living, both as a congregation and as individuals – then we need to sit patiently and wait to hear our Lord calling. And we need to continue our patient listening with each step of the journey, trusting in Christ's sure guidance even when we cannot see where we are headed, even when we cannot see the path beneath our feet at all, even when it doesn't seem like we're moving out of these rocky walls at all. Because the assurance of the Psalmist is that even when the darkness of night obscures our vision, when dawn finally breaks we will see how far we've come. And the promise of the gospel is that even when grave-clothes cover our eyes and we can't watch as the tomb gives way to open air, there will come a time when the cloth is removed and we can look back and witness how we moved from the grave to new life. For now all we need is the patience to be still and listen for Christ's call.

Stormy with a Chance of Drowning
Matthew 14:22-33

Up until the spring of 2007, I had my life neatly planned out. I would graduate from college, take a year to do jobs that were odd but fun, go to graduate school to get my PhD in International Relations, then start working for the government. Well, it seemed like a good plan, and for a bunch of years I think everyone in my life expected that that was how things would turn out. I graduated. I worked as a contractor's assistant, then as a cast member in Disney world, then as a temp. I applied to grad schools.

I got rejected.

Now wait. That wasn't on the schedule. Welcome to the spring of 2007. It was filled with crying and questioning and much gnashing of teeth as my carefully orchestrated life plan crumbled around me like a really dry, disappointing cake. I would not be starting a PhD program in the fall. I wouldn't be going into a government job by 2012 (2013 at the *latest*). And on top of all that – well, I suddenly came to the realization that I didn't actually enjoy International Relations all that much, especially not enough to do it for the rest of my life. What was I going to do? I had no plan! I had no direction! I didn't even have a stable job! The forecast for how I was feeling at that moment? Stormy with a chance of drowning. All of my ideas about how my life would go were breaking apart and sloshing around me in a tumultuous sort of way, and I was pretty certain I was going to drown in the overwhelming waters of all the decisions that suddenly had to be made.

Until my dad said four words, as we sat at his kitchen table one night, trying to get my life under control: have you considered ministry? I had not, but once he said it, I couldn't shake it. Other people mentioned it. Sermons seemed to reference it. Friends encouraged it. And suddenly there was a new direction, a direction that piqued my interest and made me excited and got me thinking and planning anew.

Have you ever had an experience like that? You're in the midst of one of life's storms – there is upheaval and maybe a bit of chaos and everything feels sort of unstable and overwhelming; you aren't sure what direction to head in next. And then an opportunity presents itself, or a suggestion is made, and even if it's not a sure thing it has a certain feeling of being 'right' to it, or it's got a kind of draw that doesn't let you go.

I wonder if that's how Peter felt out on that boat that night after Jesus fed the multitude by the seaside. Christ had sent the disciples ahead to cross the sea, while he dismissed the crowds and then got some introvert prayer time in. As the night grew deeper the clouds closed over the boat, and the rain pelted their heads and shoulders until rivulets of water were coursing down their brows and necks. Wind whipped the water into frothy waves that heaved at the sides of their vessel, rocking it violently from side to side until they feared that they would be drowned in the angry sea. Terrified, they fought to stay on course, to get to land, and just as one struggled with the tiller he saw it – something was coming toward them on the water. A shape, a figure. Some*one* was coming toward them on the water. What were they supposed to think? People don't walk on the sea. What else could it be but an apparition, a ghost? Surely this was that moment in the horror movie when the evil spirit approaches to finish the characters off for good. Their fright was certainly justified.

But Jesus said, "Don't be afraid – it's me." So now they're rocking on chaotic seas, pushed to and fro by the wind, *and* their understanding of the way the world works – namely that people can't stand on water – is in tumult. Life in that moment must have seemed unstable, overwhelming, and surely they were wondering, "what do we do now?"

Perhaps it was out of sheer desperation that Peter said, "If it's really you, command me to come to you on the water." Perhaps it was a sort of grasping at the only opportunity for safety, for salvation from drowning, that they could see. And Jesus calls. "Come." Jesus calls Peter out of the safety of the boat and onto the crashing waves – out to the very place where he would be most exposed, most vulnerable, most at risk. And it seems like Peter was captivated by that call – it would not let him go. Because he does it. He goes against every ounce of reason and steps out onto the water. And don't you wonder what those first steps were like? When he found he was *actually* standing on water, following Christ's call, it must have been exhilarating – it must have seemed like nothing could get in his way, like all was well at least for those *first* steps.

I know that's how it was for me – and maybe it's true for you too. When we take those first steps towards that opportunity – that *call*, even – that has appeared in the midst of a storm, and everything starts to click into place, it's exciting. You're doing this new thing – starting a new career or a new relationship or life in a new place – that didn't seem like a sure thing but that you couldn't walk away from, and in those first days or weeks your doubts start to recede and it's exhilarating. You feel so *alive*, like nothing could get in your way; you feel like maybe you were made for this – you feel like Peter, perhaps, doing the impossible, doing something you never imagined yourself doing.

Not too long after my dad suggested church work, I found myself moving from Philadelphia to Kansas City with grave reservations. The only job in ministry I'd really been able to find was a youth ministry internship, and I had serious doubts. I had hated middle school. I had strongly disliked high school. I had no desire to revisit those years by working with middle and high school students. But I got the job. And I started. And I loved it. I was able to connect with a bunch of the youth precisely because I had had rough years as a teenager. It was like someone – Christ perhaps – had taken jumper cables to my heart and kick-started a battery that I didn't even know was dead. Despite all my reservations, I woke up each morning loving my work, excited to be there.

But that feeling didn't last forever. I mean, I still loved my job – I still do love my job – but the farther I moved away from what I had known, away from the comfort of the plans I had had, the more doubts began to creep in – do you know what I mean? There was this voice inside of me that said, "This isn't a sustainable career. This isn't what you trained for. You aren't going to be able to do this forever. And you have no idea what you're doing – you've never counseled a kid or gone on a mission trip! What makes you think you're going to be good at this?!" And there were voices outside of me saying similar things – family members asking, "Are you really going to be able to live as a pastor? Is this really what you want to do with your degree from Stanford?" Others said, "You've got so much potential – why the church? You could still work for the CIA or the FBI!"

Moments like those, when we start to doubt the new path on which we find ourselves, when we hear the voices of friends or family or even our own internal critic saying, "you're crazy for doing this. It's never going to work; turn back;" they're the moments when we find ourselves standing on the water with Peter when he notices the wind whipping around him. Suddenly, he's not listening to Christ's voice anymore, he doesn't see Jesus standing there with arms outstretched; he's not paying attention to the miracle or how far he's come – all he can hear, all he can see, is the wind and the storm. And he realizes just how vulnerable he is. He realizes just how crazy it is to be walking on water. He realizes he's standing in the middle of a storm. And he starts to sink. In Peter's life it is once more stormy with a chance of drowning.

But Christ's response is immediate. *Immediately*, Jesus reaches down into the roiling sea and pulls Peter above the water. And then it seems that they are *immediately* back in the boat with the other disciples, the wind and the waves calming down around them.

I think for the most part, we can imagine ourselves inside this text with relative ease – we know the fear of life's storms, the uncertainty of following Christ out of the safety of the boat and onto the waves; we know what it feels like to hear the roar of the wind, the roar of doubt, and start to sink, to lose heart and faith. But we might get to this moment when Jesus rescues Peter, and we say – does that really happen for us? Does Christ immediately reach down and lift our heads above the surf?

Perhaps the better question is: do we know what we're looking for?

About half-way through my year as an intern – as we were coming up on my second summer – I was put in charge of arranging our trip to the big youth conference in Montreat, NC. I'd never planned a trip before. There were so many logistics, so much I had to organize.

It was definitely a moment of hearing the voice of doubt loudly in my ears. In the midst of it, during a week when I went home each night increasingly discouraged, a parent scheduled a meeting with me. And after we talked about her kid, she said, "you're doing such a great job. We're so grateful for you." I really didn't know how to respond, I didn't feel like I was doing a great job, so I shrugged off the complement. But a friend said to me later, "you know, maybe that was God giving you some encouragement." In other words, maybe that was Christ reaching into the waves to pull my head above water, and maybe I shouldn't have scoffed at it.

See, I think we often don't recognize those moments of grace when Jesus grabs our hand and lifts us out of the sea. I think we don't recognize them because they come through ordinary means – the voice of another person, the words of a personnel review, the beauty of nature, the event that doesn't go as planned but brings another joy. God showers us with these moments of encouragement that would revive our souls and renew our faith if we didn't brush them off as being of little consequence.

Which is why I think God provides *us* with a boat as well. Jesus put Peter back in the midst of his friends where the waves and the wind receded, and he could see the miracle of what just happened. The Spirit calls *us* together to be a similar place of shelter and of nurture. We are called to be the body of Christ for one another, helping each other see how God is encouraging us through the everyday, providing us with the grace to get our heads above water when the storms of life rage. We are called to walk alongside our brothers and sisters here, as they step out of their boats and into the unknown. We are called to encourage them, to be the voice of truth for them, the voice that says, "I can see Christ standing on the waves too, and he isn't going to let you down. You're going to make it." We are called to be like that friend of mine who recognized God's voice in that parent, and to bear witness to the ways that Christ is reaching down to pull us out of the water. We are called to be the boat for one another, so that we *all* have the courage and the faith to keep stepping out of what we know and into the uncertain – because Christ never stops calling us to face the storm and walk on water.

The 'E' Word
Mark 4:1-9; Romans 12:9-21

Having worked in Walt Disney World, it seems almost a requirement that I go and see new Disney films when they're in the cinemas, especially the animated ones. So it was that a couple of weeks ago I dutifully went to see Tangled, their reinterpretation of the fairy tale, Rapunzel. Now, like any of Disney's best animated classics, Tangled had a handsome hero, a lost princess, a fair amount of singing, a happily ever after and, of course, a cute animal sidekick. And, as is often the case, it was the cute animal sidekick that really caught my attention. Pascal, a small chameleon with a huge attitude, is Rapunzel's closest friend, faithfully staying by her side and keeping her company in the tower where she remains hidden away from the world. Watching the movie you get the sense that these two have been friends for a very long time as they work together effortlessly, helping one another without ever needing to speak a word. But what struck me the most was the way that Pascal changed colors. Like any good chameleon, I suppose, he could blend into his surroundings with ease. But unlike most chameleons, he could also change his color to match Rapunzel's mood. That's right, when she was angry, he turned bright red. When she was sad, he changed to a moody blue. And when she was in love, the blessed animal turned pink. I guess you could say that Pascal really understood Paul's words about weeping with those who weep and rejoicing with those who rejoice. And I couldn't help but think that that chameleon would make a superb evangelist.

Chameleon, superb and evangelist. Three words you don't ever expect to use in the same sentence. It is an odd concept that isn't helped at all by the fact that we have an uneasy relationship with the concept of 'evangelism' at the best of times and one that is *usually* quite rocky. It is the 'e' word that we don't often talk about, perhaps especially as Presbyterians. And I think that there is good reason for this—evangelism is a word that has gained a lot of baggage through centuries of use. It's a weighty concept, sodden with meaning, and most of us have a particular image of what it means to be an evangelist rooted in our minds - an image that is based on our own experience and reinforced by the way that evangelists are portrayed in the media and popular culture. The American theologian Rob Bell captures one of the classic stereotypes of an evangelist in his movie Bullhorn. He shows a man standing on a box on the sidewalk with a megaphone. Bell says, "As I get closer, I hear the words 'sin' and 'hell and 'repent.' And then I hear the word 'Jesus'. And he's got all these pamphlets, and he's quoting these Bible verses about the anger and wrath of God and how if I don't repent, I'm going to pay for it for eternity…this might be my only chance!" There isn't one mention of God's love. Now, this might be an extreme stereotype, but I'd wager that most of us could relate to it on some level—it epitomizes some of our core perceptions about what it means to evangelize. For example, we perceive that evangelism, at its heart, has something to do with faith sharing. It often seems to have something to do with condemnation. And it certainly *seems* to have something to do with conversion. And all of this makes most of us just the slightest bit uncomfortable. Because historically, for Presbyterians, faith has been a very private matter and our relationship with God is extraordinarily intimate—not one that is easily or comfortably proclaimed from rooftops and street-corners. And if we aren't willing to talk about our relationship with God, how are we supposed to convert people? And if conversion is the point of evangelism, how are we supposed to be evangelists? And if faith sharing and condemnation and conversion are all related, are we even sure we want to *be* evangelists at all?

All of these questions, of course, are based on a single word that has picked up a lot of baggage over the centuries. And I wonder if that baggage hasn't obscured our understanding of what it means to be an evangelist. Perhaps we are, in fact, asking the wrong questions. Perhaps the real question that we should be asking is: what does evangelism *really mean*?

In the fourth chapter of Mark's gospel, Jesus tells a short parable about a person scattering seed. Day and night this person sleeps and rises and watches as the seeds grow into flourishing plants. And Jesus says, "the person does not know how the seeds grow. The earth produces of itself." And this is what the kingdom of God is like. This is what *faith* is like. It's remarkable, isn't it? Because Christ is underscoring that there is a mystery here. God through the Holy Spirit is working in the world, is working in *us*, building the kingdom, growing our faith from a tiny seed to a large, vibrant bush. But though we may play a role in scattering the seed, in tending the ground and the plant itself, we do not know how our faith grows—God produces it of God's self. Even the very seed from which our faith originates is a gift from God. So then, if it is God who grows our faith and there is a mystery to it that we do not understand, how is it possible for us to go out and convert others? The simple answer is…we can't. As M. Craig Barnes puts it in his book *The Pastor as Minor Poet: Texts and Subtexts in the Ministerial Life,* taking on the task of converting neighbors and friends "is asking too much. *Only Christ converts.*" The creative work of salvation remains Christ's alone. So when it comes to evangelism, conversion, it seems, is not our responsibility. Which begs the question—if not conversion, then what?

When you strip away all that we have added to the 'e' word, you get back to the Greek euangelion, which literally means 'good news' or 'gospel'. At its heart, evangelism is not about condemning or converting, it's about sharing the good news of Jesus Christ; it is about spreading a love and a joy that comes from beyond ourselves, that is a blessing from God. We are not called to convince, but merely to bear witness, to share the abundant gift that we have been given in the love of God. And it is a calling that we all have in common. The thing of it is, for most of us this faith sharing bit remains a pretty uncomfortable proposition. Because there's still that issue of faith being a private matter, the relationship with God an intimate one. If sharing God's gift of love means talking about it, then we're not entirely sure that this calling to spread the gospel is one that we want to live into. So the question, I think, becomes: what does it really mean to proclaim the good news?

Saint Francis of Assisi once famously wrote 'preach the gospel always; if necessary, use words'. I'm particularly fond of this quote because I believe it captures the heart of the biblical witness in regards to evangelism. While Jesus certainly *did* use words to talk about God's love, he did it in the context of healing, sharing meals, and building relationships. And more powerful than anything that could be said, he proclaimed God's great love for us through his death and resurrection. "I came to serve," Jesus said and then commanded his disciples to do the same. And that is exactly what the early church evangelists did. Paul even wrote, "I make myself everybody's slave." A strong statement that formed the core of his approach to evangelism. For him, spreading the good news didn't *begin* with words, it *began* with relationship—with a particular relationship, in fact, that of a slave or a servant. Now for most of us, in this day and age, being a slave to anyone is a pretty foreign concept. For Paul, slavery was a fact of life, but I still think that his proclamation would have been shocking to his contemporaries. Because people didn't *choose* to be slaves; they didn't willingly put themselves under the authority of another. And yet Paul insists that this attitude, this way of life is at the heart of evangelism, this is how the good news is spread. So what might this look like for us? As Paul elaborates later in his letter to the Corinthians, being a slave means putting the will of others before your own will. It means seeking first not your own best interest, but the best interest of others. It means loving people not for our own sake, but for theirs—it means loving people *well*.

Of course, loving people is not always an easy thing to do and loving them well can be even harder. A friend of mine tells this story about how our attempts to be loving can go horribly awry. One of his friends went into the hospital just for a day to have a procedure done. He really wanted to support her when it was over, so he went to her flat when she got home and decided to cook dinner for her. Now you have to understand, this friend of mine has a great heart but is one of the messiest people that I know. And his friend, well, she's a neat freak. So when the pot that had cheese sauce in it boiled over onto the stove and he showed no signs of stopping to clean it up before it cooked onto the burner, his friend got incredibly upset. She ordered him to stop everything that he was doing and she said that she'd finish it herself. "The problem," my friend recalls, "was that I never asked her *how* I could support her. I just did what I would want someone to do for me. Turns out, we didn't want the same things."

When it comes right down to it, we've all been in situations like this before, situations where we find that the very action that we've taken in order to demonstrate our care, in order to serve, has actually done more harm than good. How did Paul do it, we ask? How was Paul so successful at *being* a slave to everyone?

With the Jews, I live like a Jew, Paul wrote, with the Gentiles I live like a Gentile; with the weak, I become weak. What Paul is telling us is that he was adaptable, he knew how to blend in. You might say that he himself was a sort of evangelical chameleon, able to take on the characteristics of the people around him. But when you really think about it, this is no small task—it's not just a matter of getting the right accent or wearing the right kind of clothes. To truly know a people such that you can live like them requires knowing something of their history and their politics. It requires a deep knowledge of their trials and their sufferings, the wounds that they still carry with them and the major events that have shaped their culture and their sense of identity. Being a chameleon isn't easy; to be successful at it you really have to listen, and you really have to take the time to put yourself in another's shoes. It isn't enough to love people generally; spreading the good news requires loving people specifically—making ourselves available to hear their stories, their needs, their hopes, their fears. It invites us to put aside our own will, our own ideas about what it means to serve and to *listen* to the people around us because it may turn out that their will and their ideas are very different from our own. But this is what it means to proclaim the good news, this is what it means to be an evangelist. Evangelism isn't about condemning or converting—it's about sharing our faith through loving. Loving particularly, loving *well*. Because in so doing, we are communicating a love that is beyond ourselves—a love so great it took on our very flesh and bone, our very life and death in order to serve us.

Chameleon, superb and evangelist. Those three words I said you'd never expect to use in the same sentence. And yet, you cannot deny that a superb evangelist is exactly what Pascal would have been. After all, he had taken the time to know Rapunzel so well that he could blend in with her—he knew her story. He could rejoice when she was rejoicing and weep when she was weeping. Yes, Pascal the chameleon would have made a superb evangelist precisely because he knew how to *love* a person *well*. And so may it be with us.

Mourning Stars
Philippians 2:12-18

This past Monday morning started off the same way they always do. I got up, got breakfast and then turned on my computer to peruse the headlines and check my e-mail. And that's when the normalcy was wrenched from my day. It blared across the BBC's website: US Forces Kill Osama Bin Laden. There was a moment of stunned disbelief, which quickly gave way to joyous relief. Because for a decade, whether I'd realized it or not, this was the man who had become the symbol for all the fear I felt knowing that I was a target of terrorism simply because I lived in the West; this was the face that I associated with those images that I'll never be able to forget of planes erupting into fiery billows as they crashed into the twin towers and men and women jumping from a hundred stories up just to escape the heat inside. Joyous relief because even though I knew it might mean next to nothing as far as stopping al-Qaeda, the ten year hunt was over and the symbol was dead. And so the words almost passed through my lips, 'Thank God.' Almost but not quite, because that was the moment that the turmoil set in. Thank God. It would have been genuine, a prayer of sorts, and that's what gave me pause. Could I really thank God for the death of another human being, no matter how cruel, no matter how much evil he had perpetrated? Could I really thank God for the destruction of one of the Creator's creations? Jesus' command that we love our enemies and pray for them came to my head. His words from the cross, "forgive them, for they know not what they do." The sixth commandment: Thou shalt not kill. Paul's words from Romans: Bless your enemies, bless and do not curse them.

It was sadness that flooded me then because we live in a world so filled with injustice and hatred and suffering that it seems at times necessary to do the very thing that goes against all that God in Christ teaches us in order to preserve peace, stand up to tyranny and protect the innocent. Needless to say, I brought all of this to my colleague Rev. Purce on Tuesday. After an hour of discussion, he posed the one question that's stayed with me all week. What do you think Jesus would have done? That was what he asked. What do you think Jesus would have done? Because in a world as complicated as this, answering that question might give us some clue as to what we're supposed to do too.

Of course, it's easier to start with that second question—what are we supposed to do—it's more approachable somehow. We see evidence of people like us in the writings of the early church, people left in a morally complex world, trying to figure out how to follow Jesus faithfully when all around them was injustice and hatred and suffering. In his letter to the Philippians, Paul wrote "do everything without complaining or arguing, so that you may be innocent and pure as God's perfect children, who live in a world of corrupt and sinful people. You must shine among them like stars lighting up the sky, as you offer them the message of life." This was his teaching for how they should live; this was his exhortation to a young church in a prosperous Roman city. They existed in a time when Christianity was not widely accepted, when the city would have been filled with those who worshipped the Roman gods and possibly even the Roman emperor, when there would have been pressure to conform to both Roman and Jewish standards and persecution for too much dissension. Paul himself was writing from prison, a fact that seems to have caused the Philippians much grief. And so how were they to live? What were they to do? Shine like stars, Paul says, offer the people the message of life. For them, with so much pressure to blend in with the people around them, what would it mean to shine like a star? It seems to me an encouragement to be different, an exhortation not to give into the temptation to conform, but to continue living counter-culturally, extending love and fellowship, spreading the light of Christ. And what would it mean to offer the message of life? To live their lives in a manner that offers the good news to everyone they meet: to rejoice in the Lord, to live life without fearing death, to embrace humility and in love be united with one another. For them, to be a star, to offer the message of life, was to demonstrate a way of living that was different from what the world around them knew, anchored in love, filled with hope and with eyes always fixed on the risen Lord. By clinging to the teachings of Christ, they could spread light to a dark and broken world.

So what about us, then? What would it mean for us to be like stars lighting up the sky, offering the message of life? Ours is a very different world than that of the Philippians. We face different challenges and different pressures. Technology has made the world seem infinitely smaller, where science has infinitely enlarged our knowledge of the universe. Christianity is no longer a fledgling group of rag-tag followers, but an established religion with 2,000 years of history. We feel the pressure to give in to consumerism and commercialism rather than emperor worship or cultic ceremonies. And the morass of moral decisions that have to be made by each of us and by our governments seems to grow ever more complex, ever more difficult to navigate as the years wear on. Not all that long ago it was normal for an elderly family member to die simply, at home, cared for by family. Now, the majority of people will die in hospitals or care homes and because of the advances in life-saving technologies, loved ones may have to make decisions about having a person resuscitated if their heart should stop or kept on life support if they can no longer breathe on their own. In 1900, the average life expectancy in the west was the late forties, meaning that most people would never have to worry about Alzheimer's or dementia. Now, many families have to confront the decision of whether or not to put a loved one into a nursing facility, as the difficulties of caring for spouses and parents grow to the point of being insurmountable. Governments have incredible technological power at their disposal and must make decisions that balance safety and freedom on a razor's edge. And, as you have cause to know perhaps better than I do, we live in a world of increasing terrorism where civilian and military leaders must make such choices as whether or not to assassinate a single man who has killed thousands before and might kill thousands more.

Not one of these is a simple issue. Not one is black and white. The Bible tells us that we shall not kill, but what does that mean when it comes to end of life care, to life support and resuscitation? We are to bless our enemies, but what does that mean when they're bombing our shores? And at the heart of the Christian message, we are to love—but how do we know if it's more loving to put our mother or father into a care facility or pass them between different members of the family? In the time of the Philippians, shining like a star and proclaiming the message of life meant clinging to the teachings of Christ. In this day and age, sometimes it feels like that isn't enough—sometimes it's difficult to see where Christ would have us go. So what are we to do?

In World War II, there was a pastor and theologian named Dietrich Bonhoeffer. He was a prolific writer with a clear pacifist theology. Jesus said that we weren't to kill; we weren't to engage in violence, but to turn the other cheek. And Bonhoeffer advocated following this to the letter—love our enemies, turn the other cheek to their aggression, pray for them. To his mind, killing was a sin and that was the end of the story. So some may find it odd that one of the things he is best known for is his involvement in one of the plots to assassinate Hitler. It was a decision with which he himself struggled, and that struggle is alluded to in one of his later works entitled "Ethics". If you read it, you find that his theology hadn't completely changed; killing someone—even someone who had committed as many atrocities as Hitler—is still a sin, period. But while his theology had largely been retained his understanding of life had changed dramatically with the war. He began to see that sometimes in life there isn't a choice between what is bad and what is good, but only a choice between what is bad and what is worse. As far as he could see, killing Hitler would mean being guilty of the sin of murder, but it would be even worse to let him live. Keeping his eyes fixed on God and yet also looking at the state of the world around him, Bonhoeffer felt that the best decision that he could make in faith was to take on the guilt of assassination in order to prevent the worse option of letting Hitler live. But he never tried to claim the moral high ground, never tried to claim that killing the German leader was a good option, simply that as far as he could see it was better than any other.

Bonhoeffer leaves us with the teaching that we must always keep our eyes fixed on both God and the world around us, never losing sight of the teachings of Christ but also never losing sight of the reality of the situation. Sometimes there is no objectively good option for us to take, sometimes there is only what's bad and what's worse, and we dare to risk making these decisions because we make them in faith, entrusting them to God. And that means that, like Bonhoeffer, we can't take the moral high ground either.

And this, I think, points to what it means to be a like a star lighting up the sky in this confusing day and age. Perhaps it is as much about the attitude we take towards the decisions that our leaders and we must make as it is about what those decisions are themselves. In reaction to Bin Laden's death a friend of mine wrote, "we must still mourn that the death of any human being would cause rejoicing." And that got me thinking, I do not know what Jesus would have done, but I think I know what Jesus is doing. Jesus is weeping. Weeping for a world where there is hatred and injustice and suffering. Weeping for a world where families and friends must decide whether or not to shut off life support. Weeping for a world where war is too common and too necessary to maintaining national security. Weeping for a world where terrorism is so rampant that a man must be shot in order win a modicum of safety for thousands of others. And if Jesus is weeping, then perhaps we ought to weep too. Yes we are stars, stars in mourning, our light born on tears that show the world that this is not the way things were created to be, this is not the way that God envisioned the world.

I do not know what Jesus would have done, but I certainly know what Jesus did. He took on the pain and the hatred and the bitterness of humanity and bore it on the cross, he broke the hold of death, of all of our expectations and rose to new life, promising new life to each of us and the restoration of all creation! It is the ultimate assurance that there is more to life than what we see around us, more for us to be striving for—that there will come a day when God will wipe every tear from our eyes, when swords will be beaten into plowshares and spears into pruning hooks and nation will not rise up against nation. And this is the message of life that we must share—that even if we have to choose between what's bad and what's worse *now*, even as we breathe a sigh of relief over the death of one man and at the same time mourn that this is not the way that God envisioned the world—that promised day will come, that bright future will be realized and each and every day we must fix our eyes on the empty cross and hold fast to the Easter promise as we strive to work towards it.

Martin Luther King jr. said "I will mourn the loss of thousands of precious lives, but I will not rejoice in the death of one, not even an enemy. Returning hate for hate multiplies hate, adding deeper darkness to a night already devoid of stars. Darkness cannot drive out darkness: only light can do that. Hate cannot drive out hate, only love can do that." So let us shine like mourning stars in the deep darkness of this night, weeping for the decisions that must be made, and let us spread the message of life that that promised day *will* come, when nation shall not rise up against nation and neither shall they study war anymore; let us spread the message of life that that promised day *will* come borne on the love of Christ, love that he extends to all of us and we to one another.

Love Is Born at Christmas
Luke 1:26-38; Luke 2:1-20

Nothing went as planned the year that Meredith Hackerman took over the Christmas pageant. She was something of a free spirit who had never had children of her own, so when she told the kids that she wanted them to learn their parts but also think about how *they* would have acted in their characters' shoes, there was a collective groan among the parents. They could see the impending disaster. But Meredith was not one to be easily swayed, and she would not relent when it came to her method of direction.

Adults helping out with rehearsal one Saturday evening began to grow concerned when the boy playing the prophet Isaiah put his own spin on the verse, "In the wilderness prepare the way of the Lord, make straight in the desert a highway for our God. Every valley shall be lifted up, and every mountain and hill be made low; the uneven ground shall become level, and the rough places a plain." "Prepare the way of the Lord," the young prophet cried, "Build a really straight highway in the desert cause God's got a car like my dad's that can't go up mountains because it's really old. Then make all the rough places into a plane so when God's car breaks down God can just fly away!"

Ms. Patti - Meredith's helper - gently corrected the young Isaiah, explaining just what "make the rough places plain" meant. As she was doing this, Mary and the angel Gabriel appeared on the stage, causing the adults in the room to take a collective deep breath of anticipation.

"Greetings Mary!" It was a promising start for the angel. "You are special! God wants you to give birth to our savior."

All eyes were now riveted on Mary. "But I'm not married yet!" she said, and the adults sighed their relief; this was at least in the script.

"The Holy Spirit will make it possible," replied Gabriel, perfectly in line with scripture.

Joy Thieves

But little Daisy Anderson, who was playing Mary, set her face in an expression that was nothing short of resolutely heroic and said, "No. No, I won't do it, because people would be really upset 'cause apparently it's against the rules or something to be pregnant and not married, and I don't want to get in trouble." She paused for a thoughtful moment before adding, "and I think it would hurt Joseph's feelings."

Mr. Ben, the Sunday school teacher, silently cheered that she remembered how dangerous it would have been for Mary to be pregnant out of wedlock – how dangerous it would have been to follow God's call. And Daisy's parents – well, they wavered between pride and horror.

No amount of coaching could get the kids back on track after that. Even once they convinced Mary to say yes, Joseph decided to leave her because he thought she really would have hurt his feelings. Daisy said that she bet Mary was really sorry, but little Michael (who was playing Joseph) said that everyone would know that she'd done something wrong, and he didn't want people to think less of him for her mistake.

Eventually, Michael's mom (using an undisclosed amount of chocolate) convinced him to swallow his pride and walk with Daisy all the way to "Bethlehem" anyway. But when they knocked on the inn's door, Billy Wilder – ever the inquisitive child and cast in the role of innkeeper – didn't offer them the stable but asked instead, "did the narrator say something about Syria? Are we in Syria? Cause on TV they said we shouldn't let people in from there. They might be terrorists, and we don't have enough food and jobs and stuff for them anyway."

Mary and Joseph stood looking at him, unsure of what to do next. And the adults weren't of much help because they couldn't quite get their jaws off of the floor. Finally, Meredith Hackerman said, "No, Billy, no one is in or from Syria, that's just one of the places Luke mentions in the Gospel."

"Are you sure?" Billy seemed unwilling to let this go, "And maybe I still shouldn't let them in because anyone could be a terrorist these days."

Meredith frowned and said, "Anyone could also be bringing good news of great joy with them."

At this point, the youngest kids – who were tasked with being the sheep – got restless. It was Ella who started the pandemonium. With the grownups distracted she started crawling under the pews and bleating, and the rest soon followed gleefully. Some of their older siblings who were playing shepherds tried to go after them, but that just created more chaos. Luke Stiller finally turned to his mom and said, "I guess I'm not going to see Jesus. I can't leave these sheep – they'll get into trouble!"

The sanctuary was abuzz with chaotic movement, but Meredith Hackerman watched completely unperturbed. She was amazed at how well the kids picked up on every possible fear in the story – Mary's fear of being in trouble, Joseph's fear of being humiliated, the Innkeeper's fear of not having enough, and the shepherds' fear of leaving their livelihood. But she supposed they heard so many adult fears on TV or from their families that this shouldn't have been surprising. She marveled at just how wrong Christmas could have gone if any of the characters had given into that fear instead of living in love. And then she wondered what the world would look like – what God could do – if people weren't so afraid, or at least if they stopped letting fear motivate their actions and decided to act out of the kind of crazy love that led God to take on our humanity in the first place. She wondered what the world would look like if people didn't let their anxiety or apprehension get in the way of answering God's call.

Meredith found herself thinking about the first time that she'd felt a sense of the Spirit's leading. She'd been in college studying to go to law school when she learned of an internship working in an orphanage in Bolivia. Something about it had drawn her, though she'd never travelled more than 100 miles from home, and the prospect of living in a different country terrified her. And she really needed a law internship if she were to finish her degree on time, so it would put her life-plan in jeopardy. In so many ways the internship scared her witless; though she couldn't stop thinking about it, she wouldn't have applied if a friend hadn't made her. When she was offered the position, she almost didn't accept it – but something in her wouldn't let it go. So she risked it and went. And she fell in love with the children. She found that the love that had surrounded *her* as a child equipped her to love these kids *well*. It made her feel so *alive*. It gave her purpose in a way that she'd never felt it before. Had it not been for that internship she might never have discovered the passion for helping that led her to change her major to social work, and that led her to a career of loving some of the most vulnerable people in their community. Had it not been for that call, she might never have discovered her particular gifts for making the love of God tangible to others.

And maybe that was what this pageant was all about in the end – celebrating the birth of Christ 2000 years ago for sure, but also reminding everyone that we are no different from Mary and Joseph and the Innkeeper and the Shepherds. There is much for us to be afraid of, but if we refuse to give in to fear, and if we instead take the risk of following God's call, then the love of Christ is born in us time and time again. If we refuse to give in to fear, and if we instead take the risk of following God's call, then our hands and our feet become the hands and the feet of Christ and new life grows around us. If we refuse to give in to fear, and if we instead take the risk of following God's call, then love is born at Christmas through us, and Christmas comes everyday without fail.

A Deep and Terrifying Darkness
Genesis 15:1-12, 17-18; Luke 13:31-35

Once, a long time ago, a great king and a humble woodcutter met while walking along a forest road. The king asked the man to tell of his life. Obliging, the woodcutter told the king of how isolated he felt working from dawn to dusk in the forests alone. The king was deeply troubled and he promised the woodcutter that he would find some way to ease the man's loneliness if only the man would wait there for the king to return. Of course the woodcutter agreed and watched with hope as the king galloped off. But as the hours wore on the man's hope turned to anxiety. And the anxiety turned to fear. How would the king accomplish what he had promised? When would the king return? How could he be sure that that man even *was* the king? And a deep and terrifying darkness descended on him. In the darkness he felt even lonelier than he had before and he was sure that the terrible night would consume him.

A deep and terrifying darkness fell on him. It fell on the woodcutter. It fell on Abraham. It's probably fallen on you – I *know* it's fallen on me.

Isn't it funny how you can read a bible passage a million times and still find something new on the million and first reading? The verses of Genesis 15 – of God making a covenant with Abraham – read like the familiar signs on an often-hiked path for me. I *know* them. I've studied them. I've read them over and over. But I don't ever remember hearing that one part of verse 12 before – the part that reads, "A deep and terrifying darkness fell on him." The words sunk their claws into my mind this week and would not let me go. What was this deep and terrifying darkness that fell on the sleeping Abraham? What was it and why did it feel like it related so well to our New Testament passage about Jerusalem killing God's prophets?

It's the timing of this deep and terrifying darkness that is striking. Abraham – or Abram at this point in the narrative – is uncertain about his future, so God makes a promise to him; God promises him that he will be a great nation. But then there is this pause in the story, this moment where God withdraws from the scene and

Abraham is left with the setting sun and the words of a promise so big it probably seemed impossible to fulfill. And that – that's when the deep and terrifying darkness descends. The thing about darkness for the ancient Israelites is that it's not just the absence of light, it also often meant the absence of knowledge. People who did not know God were walking in darkness. People without understanding were walking without light. So this deep and terrifying darkness was not just a cloudy, moonless night – it was being in a state of 'unknowing'. Not knowing how God would fulfill the promise, not knowing if God would return, not knowing if God was to be trusted.

Have you ever been there? Have you ever been in that darkness of unknowing – of being uncertain about God fulfilling a promise, of not being all that sure that God was really present, really to be trusted? There are so many promises that God makes to us – God promises us that nothing can separate us from the divine love; Christ promises us that we will have life and have it abundantly. Christ promises us that in the Spirit we will be new creations. But there's this pause, isn't there, this long pause between the moment when we hear those promises for the first time and the moment when we truly believe that God is fulfilling them? It's a pause where God seems to withdraw from the scene, leaving us alone in the darkness. It's a pause filled with uncertainty because we don't quite know how Christ is going to give us abundant life. We don't quite know what it means for the Spirit to make us into a new creation. And that's when the hope begins to give way to anxiety and the anxiety begins to give way to fear. Because it's a long pause and the darkness is deep, we begin to fear that maybe that promise of abundant life wasn't meant for us – maybe we will never know the kind of abiding joy that the Bible so often talks about. We worry that we will always be a little lonely, that we will always feel a little inadequate or worthless, that the pain of loss or depression will never subside. We begin to fear that God will never give us a sense of who we are as a new creation – maybe we will never fit in to a community as we deeply long to, maybe we will never be sure that our lives have a deeper meaning, that they ultimately matter.

A deep and terrifying darkness fell on the woodcutter, so he got to work and built a fire to keep the dark at bay. And then wishing for even more protection, he built a house around the fire. Then to distract himself from the loneliness he began to carve pictures into the walls. He built such a strong house and was so engrossed in his work that he wouldn't have heard the knock on his door if the King hadn't been so persistent. "Who is it?" he called. "It is I, the king. I have fulfilled my promise!" But the woodcutter looked around at his carvings and thought of the darkness that had been beyond his walls and decided that he had created a safe enough place for himself. So he told the king to go away. The king tried again, explaining that he had found an answer to the man's loneliness, "All you have to do is take down these walls so that I can come in." But the man found himself threatened by the king's words. After all, these walls were keeping him safe. And the carvings on these walls were keeping the loneliness at bay well enough. He couldn't imagine that the king had a better solution. So he told the monarch to go away a second time. But the king, unwilling to let his subject rot away in a shack, started to beat on the walls, trying to tear them down. This time, the man felt so threatened that he grew very angry and started yelling violently at the king until the banging stopped. And so the man remained in his shack, missing completely the king and community that waited in the darkness outside.

When you get right down to it, most of us are like the woodcutter, I think. We don't want to sit in the uncertainty of the darkness; we don't want to be left surrounded by our fears. So we come up with ways to push it away, to hold it at bay. Unsure if Christ is really going to make good on that promise for abundant life, we find our own ways of living 'abundantly.' We push away our grief and our despair, distracting ourselves with work or pretending everything's just fine by putting a good face on for the world and refusing to talk about it. We over-indulge in things that give us a fleeting sense of comfort or euphoria. We watch as our society's youth numb their teenage angst with alcohol. And we're really not so sure about that whole new creation promise either, so we search for a sense of meaning in all of the wrong places. We stay in damaging relationships because at least with that person we have a sense of belonging. We drive ourselves to the brink of insanity in a relentless quest for perfection in our public or private lives because at least then we can define ourselves by success. Or we sequester ourselves in a small sphere of mediocrity because it feels safer to be known as one who doesn't live up to their potential than one who is a failure. These are our fires and our walls and our carvings – these are the safety nets that keep the deep and terrifying darkness at bay.

I had gone to visit Mrs. Cowen. We were sitting on her porch talking as the tall glasses of lemonade between us grew condensation in the humid summer air. Through the window I could see an ordered living room with pictures of a happy family lining the mantle and walls. There was no evidence there of the whirlwind that had ripped through her life the night before. There was no sign of the hate-filled words that her son had thrown at her in his fury. "He always wanted to *be* somebody," she said, her voice slow and thoughtful. "I always told him that he *was* somebody already and that he'd see how much his life mattered if he just gave it time; if he just found his place in the world." She smiled sadly at me then, "he heard it at church, of course too – that God promised to give him an abundant life, a life full of meaning. But he was in too much of a hurry for that. I guess he just didn't want to be on the outside like he was in high school, so when he got to college and people started inviting him to parties…well, I suppose he just felt more secure when he was with that group." She was staring at the green hills that rolled away from her house, but I had a feeling that she was seeing something else entirely. "It was just a weekend thing at first. And then it was a Thursday thing too. And then Wednesday. And then it was everyday. And his grades started to go. He stopped doing all the things that made Jared, Jared. You could hear it in his voice. He was telling me that things were great, but he sounded so dull. So I told him to come home. And I told him I wasn't going to keep helping him with tuition if he didn't stop going to those parties with those so-called friends. That's when he exploded." She looked into the window, then, at the perfectly ordered living room - reliving the scene I was sure. From an earlier conversation I knew that he had called her unloving, that he had accused her of not wanting what was best for him. I knew that he had accused her of being a horrible mother. He had verbally eviscerated her. All because this woman – this small, gently-spoken woman - had threatened the lifestyle that made him feel like he *was* something, that made him feel secure against the uncertainty of not knowing who he *truly* was.

The thing of it is, while our methods of coping with the darkness may dull our fears, they also keep us from hearing the King when he's banging on the door offering us something even better. We begin to believe that the patterns of our lives are the best that we can do – we can't imagine that God's got something better in store. And because they keep us safe, we lash out when someone threatens our walls, our self-made sources of light. Even Jerusalem – poor, occupied Jerusalem – had a system in place to keep the darkness at bay; they had a system in place to maintain their identity as God's chosen people even when they were conquered time and time again. It was adherence to the law, and they built institution upon institution to make sure that people followed it. And they would not let go of those institutions even when they grew a little corrupt, a little unjust, because those institutions ensured the security of their identity. And we can't blame them, we would have done the same. But the prophets threatened that. *Jesus* threatened that. They offered a renewed relationship with God, but it meant tearing down the institutional structures that had kept them safe for so long. And that was just too much of a risk. Because it would mean facing the darkness again. And how could they be sure that it would be worth it? So Jerusalem killed the prophets, just as we would have. Jerusalem killed Jesus, just as we would have. The woodcutter vehemently rejected the king. Jared verbally eviscerated his mother. We lash out or freeze out, we push away or walk away. Just so long as our walls are safe.

But…in that deep and terrifying darkness, God met Abraham. God met Abraham and made a covenant with him. It was in that darkness that the promise was assured. In the deep and terrifying darkness that surely descended on the disciples after Good Friday, Jesus met them. It was in that darkness on Easter morning that the promise of new life was assured. It was in that darkness that the unimaginable miracle occurred.

Friends, God is knocking on our walls – these walls here, the walls of our life. Christ is waiting, longing to gather us together like a hen gathers her brood under her wings. The Spirit has a vision for us of what abundant life looks like, of how we look as a new creation. But it will mean dousing the fires that have kept us safe and venturing back in to the deep and terrifying darkness of unknowing. The thing is, we don't have to face it alone. We are in this together – and when the fears grow so deep and the uncertainty grows so wide that we start to feel overwhelmed we can remind each other of God's promises; we can remind each other of how much we are loved, we can remind each other of how much our lives matter. Because you *are* loved, more than you may ever know. And your lives *do* matter – God has given you the Spirit and thus the power to transform this world. So then perhaps we, as a community, can reach out and give others the courage to face the deep and terrifying darkness and as the body of Christ, gather them under our wings until they are ready to transform the world too.

No Lamb Cakes Here
John 20:1-18

There were some things in the Bard family that never changed. When Carolina had to move home at the age of 34, she discovered this with equal parts dismay and joy. The house still smelled of lemon pledge and pine-sol; her room still had posters of the first Harry Potter movie and books that she'd not touched since she was in High School; her mother's meatloaf was still laced with ketchup and brown sugar. But nothing remained so untouched as her family's Easter celebrations. The smell of cinnamon woke her from a deep sleep, and she knew that there would be French toast waiting on the table; her dad would be reading the paper with a cup of coffee in his hand; her mom would be waiting with spatula ready. When she finally sat up in bed, however, she was stunned to see a beautiful light pink, lace dress – complete with satin sash, exquisite white gloves and matching hat – meticulously pressed and hung on her closet door. It was exactly what she would have chosen, so Carolina briefly wondered if she and her mom had had a conversation about this particular garment. Had she forgotten them buying it together? Had she pointed it out in a magazine? Or was this shopping and accessorizing for her daughter one more remnant of Carolina's childhood that her mother had decided to resurrect? That last one had to be true, of course; Carolina's memory just wasn't *that* bad.

After the expected French toast, after the service at her parent's church where Carolina no longer felt sure she belonged, they arrived at home and her father announced – as he had always done – that there were Easter eggs to be found. It was not so challenging for the 34-year-old as it had once been, but Carolina was not ashamed to admit that she enjoyed it all the same. Afternoon brought harmonious family relaxation, and that evening her father's parents arrived bearing the lamb cake that Carolina had secretly missed more than any other part of their Easter tradition in the years that she'd been away. Frosted in delicious white buttercream and padded with coconut, with jellybean eyes and green coconut grass at the base, it was the perfect end to a beautiful, traditional Easter. And Carolina delighted in eating the entire head by herself.

Joy Thieves

It was a beautiful, traditional Easter – and it probably wasn't so different from many of ours. Oh I'm sure the specifics don't match up, but we can identify with the core features: our finest clothes washed and pressed, good food, family and fun festivities. Yes, it was a beautiful traditional Easter. But you know, there is one thing of which I am fairly certain – there were no lamb cakes on that first resurrection morning.

According to the gospel of John, this day that we celebrate with freshly laundered and starched activities started off as a messy morning of dirt and sweat and tears. We enter the story at a moment of intense grief as Mary makes her way to the tomb where Jesus' body lay. Imagine yourself in her shoes for a moment – this man whom you loved and respected had been brutally murdered right in front of you. You approach the tomb with one last act of devotion: to properly prepare his body according to your traditions. But when you reach the grave, it is open, and the body of the beloved man is gone. Can you imagine the feelings grabbing at Mary's heart and mind? Hurt, fear, panic, shock. So she runs to tell the disciples, tears streaming down her face, her garments streaked with dust. And devastated as they are, only two of them are able to muster the strength to run and see. But there aren't any answers there for them, just folded linens and a rolled cloth. And so they leave. John said that they saw and believed, but they didn't yet understand that Christ must rise from the dead. So what then did they believe? That Mary was telling the truth? That someone had taken the body? We aren't privy to their thoughts, but it's not hard to imagine that they returned to the house with just as much grief as they had when they left. And perhaps that grief is now mixed with uncertainty or even anger.

But John invites us to stay with Mary – to stay with this woman who is overcome with anguish. Without mercy, sorrow wrings the tears out of her as she stoops to see what the disciples have seen. The folded linens and rolled cloth. Only Mary sees something more – she sees two angels sitting where Christ was lying. She *talks* with them, laying her grief at their feet. Have you noticed how odd this exchange is? In every other place that I can think of where angels show up in the Bible, the human is always mystified, afraid, stunned, awestruck. There is none of that here. Mary doesn't seem to bat an eye. She answers them from the heart of her suffering. It's enough to make me wonder: does she even realize that they're angels?! And if not, does she pause to think about how weird it is that two men randomly appeared in this tomb?!

Well, of course the answer is no. She doesn't think of any of that. Nor should we expect her to. At its very worst, grief often robs us of the ability to notice the angels right in front of our eyes; at it's very worst, grief turns our world on its head and makes the familiar unrecognizable - even something *so* familiar as the person whom we've loved and lost.

Mary turns and there is a man. *We* know that it's the risen Christ, but somehow Mary doesn't see it. The despair of her situation makes her unable to see it. And this Christ doesn't appear to be dressed in glowing white, radiant and powerful – Mary thinks he's a gardener. Perhaps his clothes are stained with dust and grass; perhaps there is dirt beneath his fingernails. Whatever the case, this is not the beautifully perfect Easter morning that I think we sometimes envision. It's filled with heartache and grit and tears and the depth of human suffering. Which leads me to wonder: why do we, all these centuries later, celebrate this day with beauty and song and joy?

Well, I think the reason is actually in the heartache and the grit and the tears and the depth of human suffering. I think the reason is in this moment that happens next. Mary pleads with the gardener to tell her where Jesus is lying, and then we can imagine that she turns away from him again, searching for this body that has mysteriously disappeared. And Jesus calls her name. Mary! Mary. There is something about his voice, something about the way that he says her name, that cuts through her pain in this moment and grabs hold of her with the truth: Christ is risen. Christ is *risen*. He is no longer dead, but standing before her. And she *recognizes* him. With one word, Christ has breathed life into this profound moment of death; with one word, Christ has breathed hope into a hopeless soul; with one word, Christ has given Mary a glimpse of a bright future where death and grief and suffering are no more.

And we all long for that, don't we – an end to suffering?

Joy Thieves

The sad truth that lay beneath Carolina's perfect Easter façade, the heartache that she had to return to once Monday morning rolled around, was that she was a 34-year-old woman who had had to move back in with her parents because she couldn't find a job in the field in which she'd been trained. After four years of college and three years of grad school and even more years of training to become a hospital chaplain, she could find no hospitals hiring that could pay her a full-time salary. So there she was, living at home, forced to give up her dream and start over. She provided pastoral care to the members of her parents' church, but she was also going back to school to train as a teacher. All that she'd planned for her life seemed lost; she couldn't support herself, had to relinquish her dreams – oh and she was still single, alone. And how were you supposed to date when you were living with your parents? The weight of the emptiness within threatened to drag her down into the pit of despair.

Sometime after that Easter, Carolina was asked to visit a woman from church who had been moved to hospice. So Carolina went to do what she did best – comfort the dying, and walk beside the bereaved. When she entered the room, she was surprised to find that the woman's only companion was her son: a young man in his 30's. The three of them talked, then prayed. And the many days that followed were set in the same pattern. After the first week, the woman became increasingly unresponsive, but Carolina remained with her son in the midst of his grief. There was this connection that both of them felt, but neither spoke of. They simply sat, and they talked, and they waited.

It would be months after the funeral before they met to talk again, this time over coffee. It would be months more before they officially started dating. But in that moment when they were sitting in his mother's room waiting for death to come they both heard Christ calling their names. In that moment when both were bent under the unyielding yoke of anguish, Jesus called, "Carolina!" Carolina. Through this connection with a stranger, Christ breathed life into a profound moment of death. Through this connection, Christ breathed hope into a hopeless soul. Through this connection, Christ gave Carolina a glimpse of a bright future filled with life that would be hers. It would take time for new life to grow within her – within *them* – but in the connection that they shared they could both see the hope of the resurrection beginning to bud.

And the truth is, Carolina's story probably isn't so different from ours. Whether it's this year or in previous years or in years to come, there will be times when the beauty and song and joy of Easter are mere window dressings on a life-chapter of grief and despair. But then, at its heart, isn't that what the resurrection is really for? Christ didn't rise because life is all pageantry and celebration and perfection; Christ rose because of the mess, the heartache and the brokenness of our human existence. Christ rose to assure us that our suffering and our anguish would *never* be the period on the sentence of our lives, but that joy would come with the morning, that love would call our names and grab hold of us in the darkness speaking whispered words of resurrection hope, that the final flourish of our stories would be new life, abundant life, *eternal* life. We celebrate this day with beauty and song and joy because this day reminds us of the promise that on our *darkest* day, on that day when we feel least alive, least human, least joyful, the Spirit of God who resurrected Christ will call our name and say, "Christ is risen – and you will be too! Be not afraid, for I love you, and new life is coming."

The Mustard Seed People
1 Samuel 15:34-16:13; Mark 4:26-34

Jesus said, "the Kingdom of God is like a mustard seed, the smallest of all the seeds on earth, which grows up to become the greatest of all shrubs, putting forth large branches where all the birds of the air can nest in its shade." The Kingdom of God – it's like this tiny little seed, the kind of seed that you wouldn't give a passing thought unless it were stuck annoyingly between your teeth, the kind of seed that you'd brush off of your hands without hesitation. It's the kind of seed you'd take one glance at and judge it to be – essentially – worthless, not much to look at, not of much use to eat, and probably not capable of producing all that much either. And yet, that tiny little seemingly worthless seed – it's filled with God-given life, life that wells up inside it and causes it to grow, life that bursts forth in sheltering, spreading branches, life that gives life to the world around it as the shrub born from that nothing of a seed welcomes all the birds of the air into its shade. That's what the Kingdom of God is like.

It's a good thing that mustard seeds don't think very much. Imagine if they did…it would have been so easy for that tiny, nothing of a seed to say, "I'm just a small thing, the smallest seed of the earth. I'm no more than a speck between some animal's teeth, no more than a speck to be brushed away, surely *I* could never amount to anything." It would have been so easy for that mustard seed to forget that it was created for a purpose, gifted by God to be a blessing to so many others. It would have been so easy for that seed to believe that what everyone thought about it was true – that it was worthless, without a role in God's Kingdom. And thinking like that, it might never have noticed the life-giving power of the Lord working within it; it might never have grown into the greatest of all shrubs.

I have to say, I've known some mustard seeds in my life – and I bet you have too – they're those people who just seemed tiny and insignificant to the world, people whom the world thought unlikely to do anything of importance, people whom the world thought unlikely to give life to those around them. People whom the world cast aside as worthless.

Miss Verna's son was one of those people. When I would visit with her, she'd tell me all about him. She said that she knew her son was brilliant before he was even old enough to *really* walk or talk – and she could *prove* it. See, back in the fifties, when I'm told it was safer to let your kids wander while you were shopping, Henry – that's his name – Henry got fussy in her arms, having just learned to walk, and so she put him down while she browsed through dresses. He darted under one rack and then another, keeping it up until she was ready to go home. And when she picked him up, she was surprised to find he felt heavier. It was curious, not curious enough to stop her then and there, but when they got home, she went to change Henry and there the mystery was solved. Out of his pockets fell tons of the little nuts and bolts that held those clothing racks together. Her son had figured out how to unscrew the little bits of metal and had done so at every rack. Mortified, Miss Verna put the bolts in a bag and went back to leave them on the counter when no one was looking. Now the mortification dissipated, but pride lingered, because she knew that her son was one very smart child.

Unfortunately, the rest of the world didn't quite see the brilliance that she saw. When he was in grade school, Miss Verna and her husband got a very serious call from the school principal, asking that they come in for a visit. Sitting in that office, the couple got grave news indeed; results had come back from the aptitude tests that Henry and his classmates had taken earlier that year. And Henry – well, his scores just weren't that impressive. They were so *un*impressive, in fact, that the principal told Miss Verna and her husband that they shouldn't even *think* of sending their boy to high school – he wasn't going to be the star pupil that his two older sisters were – vocational school would be best. Well, Miss Verna and her husband were determined people and they determined that their son should go to high school and so he did. But then a couple of years later more bad news, it was his chemistry teacher this time and he said to Henry, "Science isn't for you – especially not this one. You'll never make it in Chemistry, so don't even think about being a doctor like your sisters."

Well, Henry must have learned something of determination from his parents because he went on to get a PhD. In Chemistry. And in record time. But then Henry felt called to do something more – and so he followed his sisters to medical school where he trained to be a neurosurgeon. There, God's gifts of intelligence and a passion for helping others grew, blossomed and over-spilled his life, giving life to others, quite literally saving them.

It would have been so easy for Henry to listen to his principal and his teachers. It would have been so easy for him to say, "I'm just not smart enough to get through high school. I'm just not smart enough to go into medicine." It would have been so easy for him to ignore the gifts that God had given him, to fail to see the way that the Spirit was working in him to be a blessing to others. And thinking like that, Henry might never have grown into the doctor that God created him to be.

Of course, the Bible is filled with mustard-seed people too. From the wandering Abraham and the deceptive Jacob to the fishermen disciples and the persecutor Paul – even Jesus himself. I mean, who would have guessed that a backwater carpenter born out of wedlock in a stable would be God's own son, the savior of the world? The people of his day who knew anything about anything certainly didn't see much of value in him. He was nothing to them except a threat and so to be done away with with as much haste as possible. But Jesus wasn't the first nobody who became somebody in his family. No, our Christ came from a long line of mustard seeds – including the great king David.

As our Old Testament lesson makes clear this morning, the great king David wasn't born a king, he wasn't even born all that great. He was born as no more than the eighth son of a man named Jesse, a man who didn't have any particular political ties or royal blood or great wealth or even power. And let's just say that his lineage was nothing to be proud of. You know those times when you had to make a family tree in school and draw out your parents and your grandparents and your great grand parents? I can just imagine how unpleasant those days would have been for David, if they'd had anything like elementary school in his time. David, who's your father? *Jesse*. Well, that's fine. And your grandfather? *Obed*. Yeah, that's fine too. And your great grandfather? *Boaz.* Boaz, huh? Isn't he the one who married Ruth? *Uh huh.* Ruth, the Moabite woman, the foreigner whom God commanded our ancestors not to marry? *Uh huh.* Well, that's not quite so fine, now is it? And isn't Rahab one of your great-great-great something grandmothers? *Uh huh.* And she was a prostitute, wasn't she, from Canaan? *Uh huh.* And Tamar too, right? That woman who was very nearly killed for prostitution? She's in there, isn't she? *Uh huh.* Well, you can see where this is going. Young David's genealogy reads rather more like a who's who of infamous women of the Bible than that of a king. It's easy to imagine what his tribe might have expected of him – something along the lines of criminal behavior rather than royal behavior.

So there's the prophet Samuel walking along the dusty road leading to Bethlehem with a cow trailing behind him, trusting God's word that in that town he would find the next king of Israel – and that must have taken some trust because Bethlehem wasn't a particularly big or powerful tribe, certainly not where you'd expect a king to come from! So here's Samuel, walking into Bethlehem and the elders gather round and then the whole village gathers round for the sacrifice. And you *know* that Samuel was looking over that crowd, letting his eyes take in all the people assembled, especially the sons of Jesse. And there's Eliab, head high above the rest, shoulders back, regal posture, kingly appearance. He *looked* like a king, kind of like Saul had looked like a king, and so Samuel thought – that's gotta be the one, right? *Wrong,* says the Lord. Okay, so it's not the tallest or the handsomest…or the oldest…Maybe the next son, right? *Wrong,* says the Lord. *Wrong, wrong wrong,* right down the line until there weren't any sons of Jesse left. Well, none except the youngest who was left in the fields with the sheep. And that says something, doesn't it? I mean Jesse brings all of his other sons, but not David. Jesse didn't think it was *worth* having him meet the prophet. Not old enough to be important or maybe not the right position in the order of sons. Either way, in his father's eyes – in the eyes of the nation – he was *just* the youngest son, the descendent of disreputable characters, a shepherd boy from nowhere.

But God saw something different, God saw the heart of him and knew the king he would become. And God poured out God's spirit on that young man and it grew in him, blossomed in him and overspilled his life, giving life to others as he united *all* of the tribes of Israel in one nation and ushered in the golden age of Israel.

It would have been so easy for that small, nobody of a boy to say, "I'm just a young man, the youngest of my brothers, in a village in the middle of nowhere, I couldn't *ever* amount to anything." It would have been so easy for that small, nobody of a boy to believe that he didn't have the pedigree to be anything more than a shepherd, let alone king. It would have been so easy for David to forget that he was gifted by God with a kingly heart, that God's Spirit was dwelling within *him* for the good of the nation. And thinking like that, he might never have become the ruler that God created him to be, the ruler that would unite his people.

Yes, we've known our share of mustard seed people, haven't we? But you know, if you get enough of those mustard seed people together – just a few, it doesn't take very many – you can even get a mustard seed church. They're the small churches, churches like the one I grew up in just outside of Philadelphia, churches like this one. Churches like ours, well, they were bigger once but they've dwindled now. And that dwindling process has been a hard one. Because our congregations are sort of like a family, aren't they? You get families together and suddenly there's a disagreement about how to do things and the next thing you know half of the family goes off to have Christmas dinner at Aunt Minnie's house and the other half decides not to cook at all so they go out and then there's just three or four of you left sitting around the table wondering what on earth just happened. That kind of breaking up hurts – it knocks the wind right out of you. And churches like ours, after situations like that, well, it's not hard for the world to look at us and say we're dying. It's not hard for the world to think that we're not worth very much anymore.

And it would be so easy for us to believe them. It would be so easy for us to look around at the other churches in our area, churches with thousands of members and think, "we're tiny, we couldn't possibly make a difference, we couldn't possibly play a role in building God's Kingdom." It would be so easy for us to forget that wherever two or three are gathered, there is Christ and that we too have the power of God's Spirit working within us, growing within us, and that *that* Spirit is still calling us as a church to be a blessing to others by loving our neighbors, reaching out to strangers and being a sheltering home to all.

Jesus said, "the Kingdom of God is like a mustard seed…" Well, maybe the Kingdom of God is also like a small church, a church that is the tiniest in the land, a church that is filled with God-given life, life that wells up inside it and causes it to grow, life that bursts forth, providing within its walls a home where all can dwell in the Lord's shade. So may it be.

The Furby in the Pot
1 Samuel 17:1-49

"Princeton is where I learned to be myself." My colleague, Tom, said this with the kind of faint smile that people get when they're lost in a pleasant memory. It was late in the afternoon on the day before the writing workshop at my alma mater – Princeton Seminary – was set to begin. Tom and I were having our first formal meeting, trading stories about how we came to be here in Baltimore. And he went on to tell me about a pivotal moment in one of his freshman classes. The professor had asked the students to research and write a paper about homelessness. Diligently his classmates hunkered down in the library to peruse journals and newspapers and books, but something within Tom rebelled. How could he learn what it was like to be homeless by reading a piece of paper?

Speaking with his professor the next day, Tom confessed that he couldn't write a paper on homelessness the way that everyone else was. He couldn't bring himself to connect with the issue by spending hours in the library – it wasn't his way. To his surprise, the professor didn't bat an eye at this proclamation. He said, "Then write the paper your way. If you're David going up against Goliath, don't try to put on Saul's armor. You won't be able to walk."

Tom said that conversation changed the entire course of his life. It sent him down to Trenton to experience homelessness himself, which led him to a career in community organizing, which led him to my office on that Monday afternoon.

I admit that I'm a little jealous of Tom's formational college moment. When I think back to my freshman year at Stanford, the first thing that comes to mind is the anxiety I felt every time I walked into one of the discussion sections we were required to attend after lectures. The smell of industrial cleaning spray, the chill of the air conditioning, the blue tinge of fluorescent lighting, the stomach-churning dread of knowing that my grade was based on the quality of my participation – these are etched indelibly into my memory. We'd be talking about a great classic: the Odyssey, Shakespeare, Paradise Lost, and one of my classmates would wax eloquent on the tapestry of symbolism woven into the sonnets of the Tempest or the way that Milton writes in such a way that you're tempted to feel compassion for the devil, just as humanity is tempted to sin. Hearing these impressive conclusions pouring so easily out of the mouths of other 18 year olds made the panic alarm in my head blare: "Abort! Abort! Get out now while you still can!" There were no brilliant thoughts surfacing in my brain – there was nothing halfway intelligent for me to say at all. Failure was imminent; after all, if I didn't say anything, I'd get a poor grade, and if I said any of the dimwitted comments running through my mind, I'd get laughed at. I was a fraud; I didn't belong at such a prestigious university. I didn't belong around all of these geniuses. I never had.

In my sophomore year of high school, before my elder cousins were married, the entire extended family on my mom's side got together to celebrate the dawn of the new millennium. Before dinner on New Year's Eve, I walked into my aunt's living room to find most of the family – my parents and brother included – locked in an animated discussion that involved an incredible number of polysyllabic words containing the root 'neuro' and other such scientific speak. Basically, it was like every other family conversation of my life, where a heated scientific debate raged on about a topic that I hadn't quite studied yet. One of my older cousins and one of my younger cousins, however, were standing in the kitchen staring into a pot – and as that seemed more my speed than the conversation, I made my way over. Coming up beside them I couldn't help but laugh. It wasn't dinner that they were looking at there was a furby in that pot. If you don't remember, furbies were those cute little animal toys that learned to talk and respond to you. But after the initial novelty was gone they were just incredibly annoying and impossible to turn off. I stared at my cousins.

"It was the only way mom could find to shut it up," one of them said. We giggled. So did the furby. It continued to chatter at us, and we contemplated it silently. Finally, my older cousin replaced the lid and put the pot back in the cabinet. That's where the furby belonged – in a pot by itself.

"No science talk for you two, huh?" I said, and they both sighed slightly. See, a couple of years before this we had bonded as the black-sheep-cousins. The three of us had grown up steeped in conversations like the one happening next door; our families sailed through discussions about the neuroplasticity of the human brain and the neurotoxicity of chemo meds and the neurochemistry that caused fainting goats to fall over as other families would sail through discussions about the weather or sports. And if none of those topics made any sense to you, well then, you know how the three of us felt...for most of our childhoods. We weren't passionate about science. We often drifted into our own dream worlds while at the table. And there were days when we didn't feel quite so smart as our brilliant siblings; there were days when we weren't sure we belonged with all of these scientists.

I think I had it worst of all because my brother Jon, he *is* brilliant – he always has been. In fact, he's *so* brilliant that when he was a five year old in kindergarten, he got *so bored* with the teacher's incessant dwelling on ABC's and 123's (things that my brother was already quite proficient with) that he decided to amuse himself in other ways, as five year olds often do. So he slid out of his chair and started crawling around the floor and barking. We had just recently gotten a dog, and he was very clearly channeling our puppy's energy. It was the harmless imaginative play of a young kid. But his teacher was not amused. She suggested that he be tested for the gifted and talented program, so as to get him out of her classroom, which wound up with all of us heading to a therapist for an IQ assessment.

There's not much from that meeting that I remember – I was three, after all – though I clearly recall the doctor's incredible dollhouse set complete with fuzzy animal families. What I do know, because my parents told me time and time again in the years that followed, is that I had the exact same IQ as my brother – though it never felt like that was possible to me. It felt so *im*possible, in fact, that in that first semester of college when I was sure I was going to fail, and my mom reminded me that I was every bit as smart as my brother, I told her that I didn't believe her. I wasn't ever able to keep up with Jon's scientific mind or his agility in discussion. She must have gotten it wrong.

She told me then a part of the story that I hadn't heard before. Apparently the doctor had pulled my parents aside at the end of the assessment to talk about me. I *was* just as smart as Jon, but I was also very different from him. My mom said that I was the one who sat quietly and observed everything before speaking. "Just because you don't think the same way as the other students in your discussion sections," she said, "doesn't mean you aren't as smart as they. Stop trying to be exactly the same, and be yourself!"

In other words, if you're David going up against Goliath, don't try to put on Saul's armor. You won't be able to walk.

And if you really think about our story from Samuel this morning, if David had gone ahead and stayed in Saul's armor simply because that's what every other soldier would have done in his position, he probably would have been killed. He wouldn't have been able to move; he wasn't familiar with or conditioned for the weapons that Saul used; his battle IQ might have been as high as Saul's, but it was *different*. That's why God *called* him. God called him to be king because he *was* different – different from Saul, and different from other earthly rulers.

We usually think of David and Goliath stories as those stories where the big guy gets defeated by the little guy – where the humble underdog carries the day. But I'm not convinced that that's what this passage is all about. Rather, I think the David and Goliath stories are the ones like Tom's – the ones that leave us saying decades later, "that's where I learned to be myself." And we all wind up facing Goliath at least once in our lives; for many of us, those Goliath encounters happen time and time again from our youth through our elder years. Again and again we must decide: do we embrace what makes us different from everyone else and in doing so embrace abundant life, or do we try to move forward wearing the heavy, ill-fitting, life-draining armor of Saul?

I spent most of college trying to do the latter. I held onto Saul's armor like there was no tomorrow, certain that I had to be just like my classmates no matter what my mom might say. And you know what? I hated college because of it. It drained the life right out of me. God created me to observe and *then* comment, with*out* a passion for science, but with a care for humanity in line with the doctors in my family.

Joy Thieves

God created each of us with particular gifts and passions; and the divine promise to us is that those gifts and passions will bring us abundant life if we choose them over the armor of Saul. Sometimes, though, those gifts and passions will also set us apart as *different* from the people around us. There will be times when it's far easier to shoulder Saul's armor and fit in with the crowd. Yet God created us and called us to *be* David wherever we find ourselves. God created you, and God called *you*.

So if you're David going up against Goliath, don't try to put on Saul's armor. For God blessed you with something so much *greater*.

YOLO
Mark 8:27-38

Two roads diverged in a yellow wood, and sorry I could not travel both and be one traveler, long I stood and looked down one as far as I could to where it bent in the undergrowth…

The words were printed in green script against a golden picture of light filtering through trees. The birthday card sat atop a meager pile of mail on Brian's kitchen counter – a reminder of the fact that he'd passed another decade. All of the other birthday wishes had already been stashed away in a file he never expected to look at again, but this one remained out because of the poem by Robert Frost. It had been his favorite since his mother first read it to him; he had been all of six years old and she had held him in her lap as she slowly spoke the words. He could imagine the two paths running through the forest; he could imagine the paused moment of decision-making. Growing up, he'd often returned to those words as he contemplated the choices that he had to make.

But standing in the kitchen on this birthday, Brian couldn't help but think that he'd always made the wrong decision – that standing in the yellow wood, he'd taken the wrong road. Because here he was, another decade gone, drifting aimlessly through life. He wasn't miserable, by any means; he was well paid, had a roof over his head and friends who cared about him. But he wasn't happy either. As someone had once put it, he was living but not alive, not passionate about anything – as evidenced by the box of electronic equipment that stared at him accusingly from the corner. Much earlier in his life, he'd found great joy in fixing things for friends and family, and in creating new contraptions just to see if he could. Now the box of materials and tools gathered dust as he sat listlessly in front of the television.

This was not how he'd imagined his life going. When he was all of nine years old, he and his father and sister had gotten all dressed up to see his mom get a prestigious award for her research in some kind of cancer treatment. Co-workers and students had given speeches about how inspiring it was to work with her, and in that moment Brian had thought – that's what I want. I want to be a research professor just like her. I want to be the one making a difference; I want to be the one that students love; I want to be the one respected for my groundbreaking work. Then and there he'd decided to follow in his parents' footsteps – go to the best school, get a PhD, and then teach at a prestigious institution. That was the dream. That was the image of his future self that he clung to.

But by the time he reached college, he had the sneaking suspicion that something was going awry. He'd chosen to attend CalTech – and maybe that was the first time he took the wrong diverging road. When they'd done their college visits in his Junior year of high school, it was the much smaller, much more laid back Claremont McKenna College that he fell in love with – and he was overjoyed to receive their acceptance letter. But it was the large envelope from CalTech that excited his parents. "With a degree from CalTech you can do anything.," his dad had said one night as they sat around the kitchen table, "Everyone knows that only the best go there. Well done, Brian. I'm so proud of you."

Those words had practically sealed his college fate. Brian's mom had attended Harvard, and his dad had gone to Princeton. If he wanted to be like them, he was sure he'd need a college that was as well known as theirs were. So CalTech it was.

One night in his Sophomore year, he sat alone in his room staring at the TV with such disinterest that he didn't even know what channel he was watching. His friends from the previous year were all occupied – they had so fallen in love with their lab work that he was sure they wouldn't leave even if the building were on fire. When the phone rang he knew it would be his parents. No one else called. "You'll find your passion too," his mom said, after he grudgingly admitted that things weren't going as well as he'd led them to believe. "You just need to keep looking."

By the time graduation rolled around, though, Brian had only taken one class that he truly loved: creative engineering – the art of building toys. The nights he'd spent in lab for that class were filled with bright colors, crazy sounds, and much laughter as he and his classmates concocted the most wildly entertaining contraptions that they could imagine. It had reminded him of how much he loved to build and tinker. Hours would pass by without him realizing it. He felt…alive. But it didn't fit in with the image of his future that he'd clung to for so long. There was no PhD required, no prestige in creating such meaningless objects. Never mind the fact that getting a job in a toy company wasn't easy. So he pushed aside that love, and he graduated with a degree in chemistry and was soon off to graduate school.

But now, years into his PhD, he was floundering. Not academically, of course – he was smart, and his grades were exceptional. But there was no joy in it. Everyday he got up, he went to work, he did what he was supposed to do, and then he came home, microwaved something for dinner and watched TV, having little drive to do anything else. In so many ways, his life seemed perfect – he was living the dream that he'd had since he was a child; he had everything he needed. So why did he feel so discontented?

The Sunday after his birthday, Brian went to church. It was not out of religious devotion – he didn't believe in any of that – rather, it was out of comforting tradition. Church for him was a reminder of long weekends spent with his grandparents, where he could sit quietly between them in the pew and just think. And on that Sunday, all he wanted was to think.

The preacher's loud voice crashed into his reverie with the gospel reading. And he hung on the words, "If any want to be my followers, then let them deny themselves and take up their cross and follow me." This line had always confused Brian in the past. What did it mean to take up your cross to follow Jesus? But on this particular Sunday, something clicked for him. Jesus knew that if he lived into his full identity as the messiah, using his gifts and his words to heal people and offer them hope, it would lead him down a dangerous – even deadly – path. At some point in his life, Jesus had stood in a yellow wood looking at two diverging roads…and he'd decided to take the one less traveled, the one that had no guarantee of safety, no guarantee of prosperity or success. He could have taken the other road, right? When he was a young man he could have decided to follow Joseph in becoming a carpenter. He could have stayed in Galilee and lived a quiet life. And Brian wondered, *would he have been satisfied?* No, he finally decided. If Jesus had done that, he wouldn't have been using the gifts that God gave him; he wouldn't have been living into his identity. He would have been keeping his powers to himself instead of sharing them with the world – for the *healing* of the world. And it struck Brian that if Jesus had done that, if Jesus had taken that road, then he might have gone through life feeling life*less*, apathetic, lacking energy – just like Brian felt. Jesus saw two roads, and he knew that one was safe but led to an ordinary, unenthusiastic life, while the other was dangerous and led to abundant life. He chose the spectacular – he chose to bear the danger of the cross in order to live into his divine identity, to be fully alive, and to give life to others.

In that moment, a memory floated to the surface of Brian's mind from when he was a young teenager. He'd been at his grandparents' house, and his grandmother had caught him just as he was about to take his skateboard up to the roof – only one story high! – in a masterful attempt to roll from the apex onto the backyard trampoline. When asked what he had to say for himself, his genius reply had been, "Well you only live once, right?"

And his grandmother came back with, "If you only live once, you're doing it wrong." When it was clear that this made no sense to the teen she'd said, "Yes, you only get one lifetime on this earth. But if you live it right, if you live it fully, and use what you've been given to bless others, then you live over and over again in other people."

"How do you do that?" He'd asked her.

"I can't tell you the answer. It's different for everyone. Just remember – God didn't promise you safe; God didn't promise you easy; God promised you life and life abundant."

With his grandmother's words ringing in his ears, Brian looked at the trees dancing in the spring breeze next to the church, and he realized he was once again at a road diverging in the woods. One road was safe – it was the path he'd been on for so many years. It was the path of being a good researcher but never a great one, finishing his PhD as he'd always imagined. The other road was fraught with danger – it was the path of leaving the PhD program and the image he had in his head of what his life should look like. That was the cross, to sacrifice that long-held fantasy of who he wanted to be. He'd apply for jobs that he wasn't sure he could get in order to use his creative and engineering gifts for the good of others. He'd be living his passion. He'd be fully alive. But it would mean giving up on so very much.

Brian realized that like everyone on earth he could choose either path. He could choose safe and never know what it felt like to be fully alive. Or he could choose the way of the cross – the way of spectacular – the way of living into the fullness of who God created him to be, using his gifts for the good of others.

Two roads diverged in a yellow wood,
And sorry I could not travel both
And be one traveler, long I stood
And looked down one as far as I could
To where it bent in the undergrowth;

Then took the other, as just as fair,
And having perhaps the better claim,
Because it was grassy and wanted wear;
Though as for that the passing there
Had worn them really about the same,

And both that morning equally lay
In leaves no step had trodden black.
Oh, I kept the first for another day!
Yet knowing how way leads on to way,
I doubted if I should ever come back.

I shall be telling this with a sigh
Somewhere ages and ages hence:
Two roads diverged in a wood, and I—
I took the one less traveled by,
And that has made all the difference.

Joy Thieves
Nehemiah 8:1-10; Luke 4:14-21

"Prayers for you both, on account of the joy thieves in your midst."

These were the words that a clergy friend sent one evening this past December. Earlier that day I had shared with my small group – made up of five pastors from across the country – that I was having a particularly difficult Tuesday. See, a man from another denomination had told me that I was living in sin and needed to be purified by God because I was a woman preacher and gay to boot. Upon reading this news from me, another friend from the group responded that her week was going similarly poorly. Her marriage was going through a rough patch – nothing divorce-worthy, but it was taking its toll – and she'd just gotten a call from her sister who gushed about how absolutely perfect her husband was and how romantic their one-year anniversary had been. It hadn't been meant as a malicious call, and my friend was happy for her sister, but it had also caused her a significant amount of heartache because she couldn't help but compare their situations. And so my friend, Max, wrote, "Prayers for you both on account of the joy thieves in your midst."

I had never heard the term 'joy thief' before, though it's apparently used rather frequently in some church circles, so the next time the five of us met online for a video chat, I asked my friend what had led to his appropriation of it. He smiled and said, "Let me tell you the story."

According to Max, the joy thieves struck late one Thursday afternoon just a couple of years into his first call. He was serving a small church in rural Pennsylvania that was going the way of many small, rural churches – declining in numbers, losing energy and getting older, leaving members scared and uncertain about their future together as a family of faith. To hear Max tell it, the congregation wanted to change, they wanted to keep on going, but they were getting tired, and he was getting tired too.

In a lot of ways, Matt said that the whole experience reminded him of the book of Nehemiah – or at least he thought that he and his church might have understood something of what the Israelites were feeling in that particular text. Nehemiah chronicles the return of the people from the Babylonian exile and the rebuilding of Jerusalem. It was long, hard work, and the people had many changes that they had to make (not unlike the process of redeveloping a church, though on a much, much bigger scale over a much, much longer period of time), and Max thought that after so many decades in exile, the Israelites must have been exhausted in a way that he and his congregation could only imagine. He thought that they must have had their doubts about how the future would unfold, just as he and his congregation sometimes did.

So the events of that Thursday morning felt especially Spirit-inspired, filling him with a joy that he hadn't had before. See on that morning he went to visit Hank, and Hank had told him something unexpected. Hank was in his 70's and had lost his wife just the previous year. After more than 50 years of marriage the grief was intense, and Max had sometimes wondered if Hank would ever be able to surface from its miry depths. That was why he visited the older man every Thursday without fail – to be a companion to him in his sorrow.

But Max knew that something was different from the moment he walked into Hank's kitchen. The man was bustling about with more energy than he'd had since his wife's funeral, and there was a curious chaos about this room that was usually kept obsessively neat by Hank's penchant for cleaning when the grief grew overwhelming.

"I've joined the rec center," Hank finally said once the tea was set out. This was big news, indeed. The rec center was at the heart of the town's social life in which Hank had previously shown no interest whatsoever. "I've joined the rec center, and I've met some other old fogeys like me," that was just the way Hank said it, "And I think I might have gotten them interested in coming to our church. They might even want to help out with our Friday morning breakfast."

Joy Thieves

Max recalled that he didn't quite know what to say. Friday morning breakfast was the congregation's biggest ministry, and it was the hardest to staff. That Hank was not only engaging in social activities but was also inviting people into the life of his faith community seemed a miracle.

Max was so tongue-tied that Hank picked up the conversation on his own once more. "I figure maybe God isn't finished with me after all – maybe in all of this there's an opportunity for me to serve in a new way at the rec center."

That was what stuck with Max as he drove back to the office – that the Spirit was still moving and working and acting through this grief-stricken 70-something year old. Everyone was looking for new energy and new life in the young adults; Max suddenly wondered if it wouldn't come instead through Hank. It was this thought that filled him with joy. And the joy led to a sense of renewed hope – it led to the sense that if God could do something so unexpected in this man's life, then why wouldn't God do something just as unexpected in their life as a church? And that joy-inspired hope gave Max new energy for the work that he was doing.

Apparently, that got him thinking about the line in Nehemiah that goes, "for the joy of the Lord is your strength." After all that the people had been through, and with all of the work that was still to come, Nehemiah and Ezra and the scribes and the Levites remind the Israelites that the joy of the Lord was their strength. Max thought he finally understood it – he finally understood that the joy we get from seeing God at work in the world gives us the strength to make it through the exhaustion, the grief, and the hardships of life. The way that Max tells it, that was the moment that he decided never to let go of the joy – to have the joy fuel his ministry from that second onwards.

Which lasted all of about 90 minutes. And then the joy thieves struck. They first broke into his planning meeting with the Friday morning breakfast volunteers. Something must have been in the water because on that particular afternoon everyone was crabby. One man said that he wasn't sure how much longer he could really be a part of the ministry if they weren't ever going to get any new volunteers. And when Max told them the good news about Hank, the resounding response was that these new people weren't young enough to really take on the work. When was Max going to get the recent college graduates into the church? When was he going to get people who thought that dedicated church attendance meant more than a couple of Sundays a month? He didn't say it, but Max's snarky inner voice was demanding to know when the volunteers were going to get out there and find those people themselves.

Needless to say, the meeting had left him feeling dry and weary. The exhaustion of earlier had returned with a vengeance, and any hope that his conversation with Hank had produced quickly evaporated. The rest of the day was an uninterrupted string of meetings. He had to hear about the exciting new worshipping community that was starting up on the other side of the presbytery, supported by denominational investment – which only left him wondering where the support was for pastors trying to do redevelopment. And then he had dinner with some middle schoolers who would clearly have preferred to be playing video games. Finally, after a last ecumenical meeting the next town over, he was ready to go home.

Snow had started falling while they were talking about ministry, and there was already an inch coating Max's old rear-wheel-drive sedan. He was only half-way home when the car reached a hill it just couldn't conquer. Cursing, Max pulled out his cell phone and called a friend with an all-wheel-drive to pick him up. All that was left to do was wait.

For the first few minutes Max just felt angry. He was tired, anxious about the future, and feeling inadequate. But the more he watched the snow, the more those feelings subsided. It just so happened that he'd stopped in a place where there was a giant tree off to his right. You couldn't see it, but there must have been a streetlight behind it because a halo of light caught the falling flakes on either side of the trunk. And the snow looked almost like falling stars that were caught on pine needles and tree branches where they glowed faintly. The beauty of the scene caught Max in the chest, reviving the joy that he'd felt earlier in the day, and he suddenly remembered what Jesus said: I have come to proclaim release to the captives and recovery of sight to the blind, and to let the oppressed go free. Jesus had set them all free. So why had he let so many other people in his life rob him of joy? Why had he allowed the fear and weariness of his volunteers become his fear and weariness? Why had he fallen into the trap of comparing himself to others? It seemed that the greatest joy thief of all was himself.

Watching the snow fall, he thought that there was enough of the Lord's joy in that moment to give him strength for all of the days to come. He just had to hold on to it; he just had to remember it when the weariness or the inadequacy or the grief overtook him. He just had to remind himself of what he had seen before and what he was sure to see again. God had given him enough joy in that moment to sustain him, if only he could beware the joy thieves – and not become one himself.

www.ingramcontent.com/pod-product-compliance
Lightning Source LLC
Chambersburg PA
CBHW052152110526
44591CB00012B/1952